LLPAM

BI 3995128 6

KV-386-755

BIRMINGHAM CITY
UNIVERSITY
DISCARDED

BIRMINGHAM CITY
UNIVERSITY
DISCARDED

POLICING IN CANADA, INDIA, GERMANY, AUSTRALIA, FINLAND, AND NEW ZEALAND

POLICING IN CANADA, INDIA, GERMANY, AUSTRALIA, FINLAND, AND NEW ZEALAND

A Comparative Research Study

Dilip K. Das
and
Michael J. Palmiotto

The Edwin Mellen Press
Lewiston•Queenston•Lampeter

UNIVERSITY OF
LIBRARY
SERVICES
CENTRAL ENGLAND

UNIVERSITY OF
CENTRAL ENGLAND

Book no. 39951286

Subject no. 363.2 Das

LIBRARY SERVICES

Library of Congress Cataloging-in-Publication Data

Das, Dilip K.
   Policing in Canada, India, Germany, Australia, Finland, and New Zealand : a
comparative research study / Dilip K. Das and Michael J. Palmiotto.
      p. cm.
   Includes bibliographical references and index.
   ISBN 0-7734-6037-3
   1. Police--Cross-cultural studies. 2. Police--Commonwealth countries. I. Palmiotto,
Michael. II. Title.

HV7921.D37 2005
363.2--dc22   .

                                                                                          2005044325
hors série.

A CIP catalog record for this book is available from the British Library.

Front cover design by Sarah Das

Copyright © 2005   Dilip K. Das and Michael J. Palmiotto

All rights reserved. For information contact

The Edwin Mellen Press
Box 450
Lewiston, New York
USA 14092-0450

The Edwin Mellen Press
Box 67
Queenston, Ontario
CANADA L0S 1L0

The Edwin Mellen Press, Ltd.
Lampeter, Ceredigion, Wales
UNITED KINGDOM SA48 8LT

Printed in the United States of America

Dedication

This book is dedicated to my parents, Mathura Das and Punya Das, whose love and examples have always been a source of deepest inspiration to me. *Dilip Das*

I would like to dedicate this book to Mariano and Ann Palmiotto whose character was an inspiration. *Michael Palmiotto*

Table of Contents

Preface

Policing, that most difficult of jobs engaged in by employees of the state, can be institutionalized, governed, and carried out in numerous ways, each dependent on and shaped by the historical and societal conditions in which it developed. Yet policing also shares general similarities which cross national and cultural boundaries, a convergence which is a reflection of larger changes in the global environment and of transnational police reform programs which seek to promote the democratization of policing in all states. The study of how policing has emerged to be both the same and different and how police forces engage in their work in their specific contexts, for what reasons and to what effect, has achieved both theoretical and practical importance. Comparative policing provides answers to questions which matter for scholars and provides a more grounded understanding of the dynamics of policing and the adaptability of policing systems to change; and knowledge of how and why police forces act as they do can lead to policy recommendations and better performance, as measured by the general goals any policing systems seeks to achieve more social control, less crime and insecurity, and a heightened practical appreciation by the police of the rights of people and the need for the rule of law. Comparative studies point to roads not taken, roads to be avoided, roads which could lead to better destinations, and to the criteria by which the choice of what roads to take can be made by societies and the police on a more informed and rational basis.

Yet the impacts of comparative policing studies for theory and policy will depend, as they should, on the quality of the description and analysis of policing systems and the skills and insights of researchers and authors. This book embodies those qualities. The authors, both experienced police officers who gained their practical knowledge in two quite diverse settings, India and the United States, have combined their insights gained from working in the field with a scholar's perspective gained from teaching, research and consultancy in domestic and intentional arenas and institutions. The outcome is a book which is precise in its descriptions, infused with an awareness of the practical and theoretical aspects of policing, and empathetic in its evaluations of the difficulties and the joys of doing good policing. Being former police officers themselves - a status which permanently makes them members of the international fraternity of policing - both authors were accepted by the police they talked to as insiders (as well as scholars). You never cease being a police officer, and that status, quite likely, led to greater access, openness and honesty by police officers they talked to than would have been offered to an outsider, someone who might be too critical of what the police do while knowing too little about the difficulties of the job. Police anywhere prefer talking to other, even if former, police rather than putative critics. The information on which the chapters are based can be trusted; these are not opinions and information shared by officers in these six countries which were offered to mislead and mollify outsiders.

The chapters on the six countries included in the book stress the importance of organizational and cultural dynamics on how the police view their job; the nature and character of relations between the police and the communities they serve; the capacity of the police, as an organization and as individuals, to deliver effective and humane policing; and the educational, socializing, normative and political roles and functions of policing within societies. Policing is a very practical job but also one which has tremendous implications for the stability and legitimacy of governments and the sense of justice or injustice prevalent in any society and among the various groups which comprise it. The authors capture the nuances of how the demands for social order and control and the need to be legitimate are balanced out in these six countries.

A major theme is the power of organizational culture and how the values and habits by which new recruits are brought into the ambit of thinking and acting as police are taught through formal training and the supervision of work. Each country and each police force has its own preferences and priorities in how to socialize officers to their job and the roles they are expected to play within the organization and in society - as little bureaucrats or as decision-makers having significant discretion in the streets. Police work attracts people with varied interests and values who then must be converted into 'police'. Depending on the recruitment mechanisms and levels of entry into the force or service (the label itself a good indicator of the status of the police within a society, as perceived by the police and the population), recruits will reflect and bring into the organization status/class divisions prevalent in their society. The creation of an organizational identity, and of the commitment and loyalty of all within the organization to that identity, requires major effort. Chapters describe the multiple ways in which identity and a sense of being a member of the police are fashioned and the results in terms of styles and practices of policing, of doing the work.

The first edition of the book was a valuable contribution to the comparative study and assessment of the police. The new addition adds to that lustre; discussions and analyses are more evaluative, more critical of policies which deserve to be judged more harshly, more informed by talks with experts in these countries, more detached - and that is to the good. This is most noticeable in the chapter on India which has shifted in tone and content from a personal recollection of years in the police to a much more objective analysis of the colonial origin and its continued impacts on the operations of the India Police Service; but the shift and improvement in the quality of the analysis can be seen in the other chapters as well. The book will take its place among works which anyone who claims to be informed about comparative policing and its general characteristics and dynamics will need to have read.

Otwin Marenin is a professor in the Political Science Department/Criminal Justice at Washington State University. He received his BS from Northern Arizona University and his MA and Ph.D.(in Comparative Politics) from UCLA. He has taught at Ahmadu Bello University and the University of Benin in Nigeria, and the

Universities of Baltimore, California, Colorado, and Alaska-Fairbanks in the USA. His research and publications have focused on policing systems in Native American communities in the United States and on the origins and practices of policing in Africa, especially in Nigeria. More recently, he has done research and written on developments in international policing, transnational police assistance programs, and efforts to reform the policing systems in failed, transitional and developing states. Recent publications include *Policing Change, Changing Police: International Perspectives* (editor), *Challenges of Policing Democracies* (co-editor Dilip Das) and *Transforming the Police in Central and Eastern Europe* (co-editor Marina Caparini).

Acknowledgments

Heartfelt thanks are due to K.S. Dhillon, Arvind Verma, and S. Subramanian for their comments and suggestions on the chapter in India. The chapter on Australia and New Zealand was reviewed thoroughly by Greg Newbold, Rick Sarre and Tim Prenzler who deserve thanks from the bottom of our hearts. Curtis Clarke updated the Canada chapter thoroughly and we owe him a tremendous debt of gratitude. We received great help from Robert Harnischmacher in the revision of the chapter in Germany and we would like to thank Robert profusely. Last but not the least, Anne Puonti invested her valuable time and efforts in working closely with us in the chapter on Finland. A special acknowledgement goes to Paul Ibbetson, a graduate student, who formatted the book with great skill and patience. Finally, I thank my co-author, Michael Palmiotto, for his contribution in enlargement and revision of the original book, *Policing in Six Countries Around the World.*

Introduction

This book is a major revision, expansion, and updating of *Policing in Six Countries Around the World,* by Dilip Das. The author of these revisions and expansions has been primarily Michael Palmiotto, who has put the changes and revisions, approved by Dr. Das, the original author, into place. Both authors have found themselves in a complicated research investigation involving both the positive and not-so-positive aspects of international policing. *Policing in Canada, India, Germany, Australia, Finland, and New Zealand: A Comparative Research Study* is a partial account of the authors' search for capturing the profiles of the police in six countries through an observation of the aspects that attracted us as most interesting. As authors, we have been motivated to find also some ideals in policing.

As former police officers, we have always been interested in executive management. Our interest in policing includes: the role of the executive, the organizational issues such as leadership, organizational autonomy, morale, responsibility, liaison with the public, relations with minorities, politicalization, corruption, and the powers and effectiveness of the police. Our research has included these issues.

The six countries on policing that we have written about have some similarities but to a great extent are different. Several of these countries, India, New Zealand, Australia and Canada have been influenced by the English approach to policing. Since these countries were one time colonies of the British Empire it is no wonder that after centuries of English rule many of the customs, traditions and expectations of the British has been adopted by their former colonies. However, even though all these countries came under British rule there are differences in their culture and values systems were not eliminated by the British rule over them.

Despite the fact that the British ruled India for several centuries, it should not be forgotten that India was a great civilization and had a great culture before becoming a colony of the British. The British ruled India for several centuries and established a policing system that has long since been integrated into the India administration of justice process. When the India policing system is examined remnants of British influence can easily be found in the training, rank structure and policing philosophy but the Indian police can not be understood without placing them in the framework of Indian culture, her history, economic, politics and, other unique characteristics.

The British settled the countries of Canada, Australia and New Zealand. They did not regard the inhabitants they found, when they arrived, to be civilized by their standards. The alien rulers looked down at the native people in these countries as inferior. This is reflected in these peoples being called aboriginals. The English settled in these countries, took control of the lands they wanted and developed these countries according to the British free market system. However, the legacy of the British colonialism was the transformation of the native people as second-class citizens who have been a source of anxiety for the police established by the rulers. It has taken centuries to wipe off the consequences of derogatory treatment handed over to these people.

The Canadian government has been emphasizing the policy and practice of multiculturalism. In the enforcement of laws the Canadian police are influenced by the policy of multiculturalism. The police commitment towards multiculturalism has been internalized. In addition to the aboriginal population Canada has seen an increase in immigration from other countries. In the twenty-first century the Canadian police must deal with a visible minority.

While Canada, where the police are not an object of violent antagonism, looks peaceful, Australia presents a picture of turmoil which can be traced to her history. In the nineteenth century Australia was a penal colony for the British. Aboriginals, native people of Australia, were considered "Stone Age" people without rights. In the latter nineteenth century, laws restricting immigration of certain races were passed. The idea was to keep Australia "white." In the early twentieth century Australia established a federal form of government. This is reflected in a federal police agency along with individual states having their own police agencies. Australian police continue to be dogged by the turmoil that has been a historical legacy.

It was not until the last quarter of the nineteenth century that New Zealand was unified politically by the British. New Zealand has a small population and was founded upon a belief in equality, making it classless society. The New Zealand police are respected by the people of New Zealand and are free from corruption. In the late nineteenth century the New Zealand police adopted a great deal of the philosophy and reforms of the English police. The police of New Zealand have a tradition of being non-political and play a role in making recommendation on laws to parliament.

The Finnish police are the fifth police agency to be discussed. The historical background of the Finnish police is Scandinavian. The Scandinavian countries are similar in social and political systems. Finland has a centralized police structure that continues to be dominated by its Russian bureaucratic heritage. Finland has a population of five million people with a very small minority population. The Finnish police respect the individual rights of its citizens. For decades Finland has been a country with a small crime rate.

The German police organizational structure consists of an elaborate hierarchy. Their police duties are primarily geared to the preservation of law and order. They emphasize crime control. In the early 1990s the two Germanys, East Germany and West Germany, became one country. With the fall of communism in the Soviet Union, the country dissolved and the east European countries under its control were given their independence. The Berlin wall which separated east Berlin from west Berlin was torn down and the city became one. West Germany, at the request of the East Germans, absorbed the other part of Germany. This had an effect on the East German police. They had to be absorbed into the German police structure. Keep in mind that the West Germans were calling the shots. West Germany was the wealthy country while East Germany was the poor country. Also, West Germany was a democracy while East Germany was a dictatorship under communalist rule. With East Germany being integrated into West Germany to make one Germany the East Germany police were disbanded. Many East German police lost their positions. The authors of this book are not in a position to judge the correctness of the elimination of police positions. The uniting of Germany into one country was a difficult task, economically, socially and politically. The wealthy Germany, West Germany, had to carry the burden for the poor Germany, East Germany.

Although we have studied policing in many other countries, we have included only the research completed in six countries in this book. In selecting some interesting aspects of policing in India, Australia, New Zealand, Canada, Germany and Finland, we have been prompted by our desire to discuss issues connected with our interest as described above and these interests were generated by frustrations and hopes we experienced as former police officers. Our police experience motivated us to observe with greater interest certain aspects of policing that were especially attractive to us in these countries. In India, for example, we were drawn to the rigid hierarchy of the police system, the gigantic problems of disorder and the related problems, while the innate integrity of the police in New Zealand attracted our attention. Politicalization of the police in Australia dominated our observation of the police in that country, and we found multiculturalism of the Canadian police an aspect of absorbing interest as we wrote about that country's police. German police stood out in our minds for their

4

rigid adherence to laws. In Finland we found it fascinating that the police were bureaucratic but respected by the people as an honest public institution.

In writing these chapters we have tried to avoid value judgments but perhaps our accounts are colored predominantly by our subjective inclinations. We have been in a sense travelers in the bewitching land of policing rambling along the paths we found rich and alluring. This book was not written with the intention of discovering anything in particular about policing in these countries. Our goal was to write an accurate but at the same time a description of police in these six countries covering those aspects that attracted our interest. We hope that we have succeeded in producing profiles of policing that others will find equally attractive.

Chapter 1

The Curse of Colonialism and Politics of Scarcity

The Indian Police

Introduction

India was victimized by colonialism for more than two hundred years. All institutions which the British governments built were products of an alien culture, the British colonial system of values. The British rulers created a unique environment in colonial India, in which everything English and Western was accepted as superior. The exploitation of the ruled by the rulers was the norm of the colonial regime. The Indians were the white man's burden for those of Her Majesty's colonial servants who were condescending. In that cultural environment, many Indians condemned all that was Indian. Their admiration for Western culture was an ideal for an ambitious Indian youth, it was a pursuit in education for children in middle class homes. Often Indian children, whose parents and grandparents served the British administration, were told from a very early age how superior the British civil servants were in character, values, and behavior. Those children often grew up with an unrealistic idea that one must turn to the affluent and industrial societies of the West to learn all that was worth learning. Colonialism represented a tendency for apish imitation, a lack of self-pride, a denigration of patriotic spirit and an absence of commitment on the part of the rulers to the ruled.

Unfortunately, although India has been an independent country for the last 50 years, the alienation between the bureaucracy and the citizens has not ceased. According to an Indian observer of the police (Vadackumchery, 1999), it is only in 1993 that the Protection of Human Rights Law became the nation's law, more than four decades after declaring itself a constitutional democracy. Does this curse of colonialism continue? Colonialism also let the country get mired in dire economic straits. Although India has progressed economically tremendously, the country is one of the poorest nations on earth. Amy Waldman (The New York Times, December 2, 2002, P A3) says that India is a country "that has modernized in many fronts but that remains desperately poor". Scarcity resulting from poor income and wealth has resulted in intense competition for scarce goods and services not only among various ethnic groups but also among public officials as well as among government institutions. This politics of scarcity also generates cutthroat struggles for the loaves and fishes of official positions accompanied by rivalries, backbiting and jealousies among bureaucrats.

Among the various parts of the Indian police, the Indian Police Service (IPS), a national civil service that in the British period in India was called the Indian Police (IP), was steeped in the most direct and strongest tradition of British imperialism. During the initial period of colonialism the IP was manned only by British officers. The observer author of the book narrates that he and his colleagues serving in the different Indian civil services including the police in the late sixties could not escape the curse of colonialism although the British left India in the late forties. True, the country, people, and civil servants have changed during the last five decades but it seems to be also true particularly in the case of Indian administration that more things change, the more they stay the same. The colonial administrative apparatus has been done away with but not the spirit of colonialism. It is argued that the curse of colonialism in conjunction with the politics of scarcity has been haunting India.

The chapter is a perspective on the police in India through an account of the IPS. It is based primarily on the experience of the observer author who became a Member of the IPS in 1965. Its primary focus is the IPS officer, his training, role and, unique potential. Although the experiences of the 60s are rather

8

dated today, it must be added that the observer author has maintained close contacts with the Indian police. He has also studied the changes in the police as a field observer till 2001. Close contacts and the actual observational studies have enabled the authors to claim that the observations and comments rooted in the experiential perspective of the late sixties and the seventies are true even today. Further, this account has been read by several IPS leaders (Dhillon, Dutt, Subramanian and Verma, all recently retired or serving members of the IPS) who have found it applicable to the present Indian police situation. The experiential observations and accounts are also supported by the existing literature on the Indian police.

The IPS: An elite but yet not an elite service

Bayley (1966) says that the "IPS does qualify as an elite service." He further adds "to talk to an IPS officer is, in a vast majority of cases, to talk to an educated man." Members of the IP have provided few "vivid accounts of their own share in the maintenance of law and order" (Griffiths, 1971). Unfortunately, there has been a "comparative neglect" by historians in recording "the loyalty and courage of the Indian policemen of all ranks" who were ably "led and inspired by what is technically described as the Indian Police (IP)" (renamed the Indian Police Service (IPS) after the British left India in 1947). Griffiths adds that "the officers of that service will rank high amongst the small body of British servants of the Crown who helped modernize India." Although individual accounts are scarce, the importance of the IPS is well-documented (Brass, 1990; Cohen, 1988; Jeffrey, 1986; Morris-Jones, 1964).

The IPS is one of the civil services of the country such as the Indian Administrative Service (IAS, which was formerly, Indian Civil Service, ICS), the Indian Foreign Service (IFS), and the Indian Revenue Service (IRS), etc. The minimum educational requirement for the IPS is a college degree, a baccalaureate, in any academic discipline: it may be anthropology, biology, chemistry or

9

computer science. The Indian requirements are very liberal, unlike those in Japan, Germany, and Finland, where degrees in law are more common for those occupying higher police positions. As mentioned before, only Englishmen from Great Britain were hired for the IP. Around 1920-21, a few Indians were also permitted to enter this exclusive Englishmen's preserve. At present, the IPS is a covenanted civil service under the All India Services Act. The entrance examination to the service is administered by the Union Public Service Commission on behalf of the President of India. This Commission is also responsible for determining the eligibility for entering the IAS, the IFS, and the allied civil services.

Young university graduates are hired to the services through Combined Competitive Examinations. The requirements for entry into all these services, however, vary. The successful IPS candidate is required to qualify in the least amount of tests which consist of a series of papers on various academic subjects. The requirements for the IAS and the IFS are more stringent. The members of the IPS get lower salaries, more limited chances of promotion, and lesser privilege than those who qualify for the IAS. An IPS member is allowed to qualify for the IAS by further competitions. Most IPS members come to this service, having failed to be selected for the IAS (Bayley, 1969). The method of selection by default is not conducive to building pride and confidence in the IPS members, and it has negative implications for the police in India.

Frictions between the IAS and the IPS and their predecessors — the ICS and the IP — have been historical. Donnison (Quoted by Hunt and Harrison, 1980) states:

> They were of course a particular, and particularly sensitive aspect of the relations of the I.C.S. with all other services... It enjoyed better pay and pensions... exercised more powers and more responsibility... It was recruited from university graduates (Oxbridge graduates at that) and, by and large, from a higher social stratum.

Donnison adds "on formal occasions the service took precedence over all other services." Some members of the service and "their wives were not devoid of a certain condescension towards those in other services ... it becomes clear why the ICS were often referred to, with some jealousy and resentment, as 'the heaven-born'."

The IAS members play very important roles in the country's administrative structure. The principal administrative divisions of a government in a state in India are departments. These are headed by ministers who are elected. They are members of state cabinets of ministers which are headed by Chief Ministers. At the level of the Government of India, the administrative divisions are known as ministries. Each ministry is headed by a minister who is part of the Cabinet of Ministers headed by the Prime Minister. The official immediately below the minister at the state level as well as at the national level is a permanent civil servant who is always a member of the IAS. Further, the states in India are divided into districts. The IAS officers are also District Magistrates, heads of the district administrations. Besides they occupy other important administrative positions at state and national levels. Spangenberg (1976) describes the importance of the district administration and the permanent secretaries as follows:

> Districts ... had traditionally been considered as the core of British administration. The fundamental features of district administration had been inherited from the Mughal apparatus for the collection of revenues ... Secretaries to governments were pivotal figures in the formulation of the policy.

Subdivisions are parts of districts. The immediate administrative head of the subdivision is also generally a young IAS officer designated as Subdivisional Officer. He had higher responsibilities and greater prestige than his young IPS counterpart, the Subdivisional Police Officer.

During the British *Raj*, it was not possible "to think of the I.C.S. District Officer ... without thinking of the Indian Police (I.P.) District Superintendent of Police ... in this team the I.C.S. man was only 'primus inter pares'" (Hunt and

Harrison, 1980). The uneasy relationship between the District Superintendent of Police and the District Magistrate was not as serious because of the special bonds that had existed among a small group of His Majesty's colonial civil servants. The relationship was "an arrangement peculiarly English which worked on the whole very well" (Bayley, 1969). This is not to deny that membership in a service that was conspicuously inferior can build into the officers of the IPS a feeling of being a pariah (Radelet, 1986; Van Maanen, 1978; Banton, 1964). Under British rule, the police had no professional autonomy; they were subordinated to the district magistrates. Viceroys in New Delhi represented the British monarch, and the District Magistrate was the little monarch in his district. Traditions of the monarchy were pervasive throughout the whole bureaucracy. Under a power-hungry or indiscreet District Magistrate, subordination was extensive. Police subordinates, who are administratively under the control of the police chief, can be given orders directly by the District Magistrate. In the districts, the police chiefs are required to work under the general control and direction of the District Magistrates belonging to the IAS. Accordingly, the Director General who heads the State Police Department is subjected to the orders of the IAS bureaucrat who heads the Home Department in the State Government or his IAS superiors.

It is interesting that a small group of IPS officers are given a few assignments similar to those of the IAS members. They may be given the status of a permanent secretary to the government at the national or state level or other conventionally non-police positions. For example, in the national administration in New Delhi there are police officers who occupy high-level administrative positions in the Ministry of Home Affairs in the Government of India. There is a perception that these prestigious assignments are offered to assuage the feelings of the IPS. This practice is said to be a reflection of "the reconciliation system" (Bretcher, 1969), a strategy of India's political leadership which is a "compromise among competing political and interest groups ... characterized by pyramidal authority structures, multiple loyalties, the acceptance of compromise, pluralism and ideological diffuseness."

Although appointed by the Government of India, members of the IPS and the IAS are deputed permanently to the states for their entire career unless the national government asks them to work in any of its establishments. Even then the member can join the national government only if he is permitted to do so by his state government. His service terms are primarily determined by his state except in matters of discipline where the approval of the national authorities is required to be obtained by the state government. These terms are expected to ensure his independence from the local government. At least one half of all officers are not sent to their home states, to ensure national integration and arrest the obvious lack of cohesion and unity in the country. Morris-Jones (1964) observes that "All-India Services have come increasingly to be seen as a great force for national integration, in many respects more reliable for this purpose than all-India political parties."

Even under the British *Raj,* policing was the responsibility of the state governments (1). In India policing commonly denotes the police service delivered through police stations spread over the length and breadth of a district. There are police organizations in the employment of the Government of India like the Central Reserve Police and the Border Security Force. They have also been described as the "elite force" (Wolpert, 1982) and "the new elite arm" (Wolpert, 1982) of the Indian government. These are Special Forces. The members of the IPS start their careers in districts, although afterwards they may serve in the police units controlled and operated by the Government of India. The IPS is like the elite police service in Japan where the senior positions in the Prefectures and the National Police Agency in Tokyo are manned by the same pool of elite officers who graduate from National Police Academy.

The IPS officers, and as a matter of fact, the IAS officers, too, have frictions with the officers of the Indian army in their relationships. The observer author could recall how during his district service his Superintendent of Police shouted at an Army Captain for not saluting him. The former felt that the Army Captain did not pay compliments to the police officer by saluting him although he wore the insignia of a Colonel. As a semi-military organization, the police followed some military manners and customs, but they were not as strict in these matters as the army. Army officers apparently lacked respect for the police. IPS officers enjoyed rapid promotional opportunities and considerable responsibilities quite early in life, which made army officers jealous. Differences among bureaucrats on matters of power, prestige, and privileges are an unfortunate but everyday reality in India (Cohen, 1988; Spangenberg, 1976). Perhaps in India, a country of traditional caste hierarchy, these differences are more intense and self-defeating.

Training of an IPS officer

For a few months all members of the IPS, the IAS, the IFS and other national civil services undergo training in a course, called Foundational Course, conducted at the National Academy of Administration. They attend courses on political, economic and cultural issues concerning India. Through combined training programs, the members of the nation's top civil service (recruits) are exposed to one another so that they can interact collegially among themselves and learn to work together professionally in the future. India's enormous diversity in culture, religion, race, and economic development was taught in the Foundational Course at the National Academy of Administration to familiarize the budding administrators with a broad knowledge of the nation's challenges. However, the appreciation of India's gigantic complexities was sought to be implemented through routine and conventional methods. Teachers and teaching methods were uninspiring to the young civil servants.

There was also a lack of social interaction among the members of the various services which prevented them from building camaraderie. This may also be attributed partly to India being a class-based, caste-ridden society. Class distinctions, which may operate in subtle and discreet ways in Western societies, are not covert in India. Many members of the IPS hobnobbed with their IAS counterparts during the Foundational Course, but the atmosphere appeared generally to have prevented the creation of a climate of mutual appreciation and collegiality among the recruits. The obvious differences in importance, status, salary, power, and privileges between the IAS and other services prevented the National Academy of Administration fostering in IPS members a spirit of comradeship with IAS members. Often unease, diffidence and apprehension showed in the IPS trainees because the IAS was accepted as a superior service. In the Foundational Course the National Academy of Administration could not avoid the culture of the traditional caste system.

The observer author recalls a member of the IAS telling another how he would engage "his" Superintendent of Police in "his" district to do what he thought he would like the latter to do. As an IAS trainee, he was aware of his higher caste in the administrative hierarchy. Ironically, the future discords and uneasy relationships between District Magistrates and the District Superintendents of Police were born in the Foundational Course. It has been mentioned also how inadequate the intellectual aspects of the course were in regard to meeting the objectives of inter service collegiality and understanding.

Professional police training

After four months in the Foundational Course, the IPS members enter the IPS academy for one year long basic course. Upon entering the academy the recruits' hair was immediately cut short and they were outfitted with various uniforms including physical training shorts, parade outfits, class room uniforms, and dining clothes. This process was a ritualistic drama, which reinforced for the trainees their new career. The trainee's new career requires him to be different than what he had been in his pre-police life and what he might have expected in a civilian job. Emphasis would be on spit and polish, appearances and

15

appropriateness (Harris, 1973). Police trainees learned to be intolerant of anything sloppy.

Training consisted of much physical exercise including compulsory games like football and hockey. The physical regimen was vigorous. Everyday the trainees would 'fall in' in front of their barracks at dawn. They would be marched by a physical drill instructor to the parade ground. These instructors were tough people from the Indian Army or armed police battalions (2) which are Indian versions of the French *Gendarmerie* or the German *Bereitschaftspolizei*. The trainees would have to endure rigorous physical workouts which included riding, marching, and shooting. Instructors would publicly scoff at 'sissies' and use choice slang used in the army training ground. The derision for poor physical performance made the trainees strive to excel in physical skills. Trainees were often told that the IAS officers were soft, weak and only fit to be pen pushers or glorified clerks. In the vastly different cultural context of this IPS school, apparently the same stress "by the staff and visiting lecturers…on construction of a feeling of specialness … a 'we are the best' syndrome" occurred as it also occurred at American police academies (Harris, 1978). "The disparagement of the elite professions found willing ears among the recruits" of the IPS. Policing was perceived in classrooms and parade grounds "as the most noble and sincere profession." To build the IPS ego, trainees were made to realize how much they could take. Physical prowess was glorified to distinguish IPS from the IAS. Horseback riding, which was considered important for imbibing officer-like-qualities demanded skills; many probationers dreaded it. While at the training academy, the observer author noted a colleague falling from a horse and receiving a serious injury. So strict was the regimental discipline that trainees were not allowed to look at a fallen rider. They were told by the instructor that in the best tradition of the British Army, officers on parade did not make any movement other than what they had been commanded to make.

Current IPS training, however, is more academic and thorough than it was in previous decades. Now, trainees receive instruction in criminal law, criminology, police science, investigation and administration of the police. They also attend classes on concepts and practices of management along with community relations. This is how the observer author was briefed during his recent visit by the Director of the National Police Academy (Raj Gopal, 2001) who coincidently happened to go through their police professional training together with the former and was fully familiar with what took place then and now.

Law was the most important academic subject. Sociology, management, or ethics classes were conspicuous by their absence. Forensic science was included to a limited extent. Training classes were devoted mostly to law courses and taught by police officers. In classes no discussions occurred on sociology or philosophy of law; law was taught as series of statutes to be cleverly memorized and adopted for use in police work. Future police leaders acquired the notion that law was an instrument of police authority; it was not a fundamental course of study to be pursued by thoughtful practitioners of enlightened policing (Skolnick, 1967). Other courses consisted of lectures on criminology, forensic sciences, and police procedure. The law curriculum also included the study of special criminal statutes that the British made in disregard of human rights, namely, The Criminal Tribes Act, which labeled a few Indian tribes as "inherently criminal and dangerous" (Arnold, 1985). Trainees were told why these tribes were subjected to harsh restraints particularly in regard to not allowing them freedom of movement outside their jurisdictions.

Unfortunately, the observer author does not recall many role models among the instructors. What seems to have made a lot of impressions is that the trainees were constantly made aware of how to dress properly for different occasions. As mentioned above, there existed much stress on shined shoes and on visible ironing of proper creases in uniforms. For proper grooming the trainees were required to appoint personal bearers to look after their clothes, shoes, socks

17

and other accessories. Conformity to what was considered proper was the focus of the professional police training. Anyone who violated the rules was immediately singled out by instructors and the trainee was publicly castigated. Even minor violations were not overlooked. A colleague of the observer author (batch mate as the popular term in India is) had written in green ink a letter to an administrator at the training school. Next morning the cadets were told in solemn and mocking tones that in official correspondence only black and blue ink could be used. Green ink, the trainees were told, was suitable only for writing love letters. It was the need for complete subordination that was projected every moment to the trainees; subservience was stressed by such words as "discipline," "dependability," and "OLQ" (Officer-Like Qualities) etc. Perhaps the Criminology instructor of the observer author summarized what worked best for the police in India. On the first day of his class, he told each IPS class that a police officer who wanted to avoid trouble would listen to his superior at 'attention,' salute him 'smartly,' with palm shaking and heels clicking, receive his orders with demonstrated humility, and do a 'quick march' out of the room while subserviently saying, 'Very well, sir.'

At the mess where trainees ate, there were regular mess nights, dinner nights, guest nights and other special occasions. Although trainees could eat with their fingers at home and wear *dhoti* or loincloths there, they had to become Westernized gentlemen, skilled in so-called genteel manners and etiquette. The trainees learned the proper use of cutlery, correct way of chewing food, and gentlemanly conversational style at meals. They were to become the elite, *Burrasahibs,* and their training was to be a passport to a so-called sophisticated world of 'officers.' The trainees were not reminded of the basic Indian values; the emphasis was on making them westernized gentlemen. The Western manners and customs in which the trainees were initiated into were the hallmarks of the officer culture in India. For most trainees, eating habits and manners, dressing customs and social etiquette meant being native at home and Westernized in official events. The bureaucratic culture of officialdom is alien to the traditional Indian culture. The IPS trainees had to learn to behave like Westernized bureaucrats while 'Indians' at home. Their double lives were not without conflict. Halbfass (1988) observes that "India has been an object of European interests of political domination, economic exploitation, religious proselytism, scientific research and historical understanding." There seemed to be an irony in the practice of European manners and customs instilled in Indian Officers. True, this emphasis is perhaps necessary because these are the international standards of social manners.

The underlying stress in acquisition of an all India attitude, which was the most obvious objective of the Foundational Course, continued to be an important concern the professional police training period too. Trainees tour the country on a Bharat Darshan, "See India" trip, to acquire familiarity with the country and its police. They meet many police leaders in various parts of the country and learn about the similarity of police structures in different states. Further, trainees camp at an Indian army cantonment in the border regions to become acquainted with the problems of army personnel who leave their families alone at home as they serve in operational areas. Because army families may face harassment from unscrupulous neighbors or relatives, particularly in the villages where government presence is not strong, the trainees are made familiar with the problems of army personnel in civilian spheres.

On the job training

After receiving intensive training the recruit is sent to the states to which they are assigned (Diaz, 1994: 196-197). The observer author was sent to the State of Assam. The first year in the state is spent in field training in a district. As mentioned above, the real police work is in the district where an IPS trainee receives field training. This period of training is primarily utilized as a period of understudy for a practical familiarity with the responsibilities, challenges and work of the District Superintendent of Police who oversees a District Police Office. Although there may be minor differences how these offices are organized, generally, a District Police Office in most states is composed of the Superintendent's Confidential Branch, the Crime Branch, the Special Branch, the General Branch, and the District Police Reserve (3). The trainee was required to learn the various activities of these branches.

The District Police Confidential Branch was directly under the supervision of the Superintendent of Police. It handled matters of a confidential nature about political affairs and security. Such matters consisted of reports about individuals considered dangerous to public security, arrangements for visits of the Prime Minister and the President of India, results of reports of inquiry, and annual confidential records of certain categories of officers. It was important for the Superintendent to know where all politically dangerous persons were located. In India the police tradition for spying perfected by the colonial masters did not end with the British *Raj*. Spying performed by the Confidential Branch was in addition to the responsibility for political intelligence handled by the District Special Branch. A visit by the Prime Minister of India to a district was the most important security matter for the Superintendent of Police. All instructions were issued by the Government of India from New Delhi and the Superintendent was made personally responsible for strict compliance with all instructions.

Inquiries were part of the Superintendent's job. Sometimes signed but generally anonymous letters against police personnel or civilian members of the District Police Office were received by the Superintendent. Allegations against members of the District Police made to the District Magistrate, and other top police administrators were invariably sent to the District Police Chief unless they contained allegations against the Superintendent himself. Anonymous letters containing allegations against subordinates were investigated. Many of these letters were written out of vindictiveness and jealousy and were used to coercively control subordinates. The press was vigilant about the police in India as elsewhere. Some press correspondents considered that publication of allegations was a form of public service.

Confidential reports of the performances of all subordinates of and above the rank of Sub-Inspectors were made annually. The reports were made conscientiously, because no examination for promotion of subordinates was given as it is in other countries. Ironically no performance records were kept for Constables, because they had no chances of promotion. That Constables were not generally entitled to promotion in sharp contrast to practices in France or Germany where the lowest ranking officers could take examinations for higher posts. In India a Constable or any other non-IPS officer was unable for various reasons to take an examination to enter the Indian Police Service on the basis of the experience in the service of policing.

The gathering of intelligence about subversive political groups or the activities of political parties in opposition was an important part of the district police work. Depending upon morality and ethical standards of the politicians who controlled the government, demands made on intelligence varied. When the observer author served his term as Superintendent of Police, the State Home Minister indicated to him how even falsified reports about his political opponents were welcome to him. Intelligence was collected through plainclothes police officials directly or through contacts and secret agents known as 'sources.' Sources were paid either on a regular monthly basis or upon the completion of reports on special tasks given to them. After Independence, the gathering of secret information, an essential activity for an alien government, was retained and grew in importance. As a matter of fact, the intelligence role of the police had been gaining in importance. The Indian bureaucracy before Independence was the basis of a stable, secure and fundamentally peaceful country. The colonial bureaucratic apparatus which served the British so well had passed the test of time, and the post-Independence leaders who were mostly lawyers by profession, did not want to weaken its form and legitimacy in the absence of a viable alternative (Arnold, 1986; Kumar, 1989; Kohli, 1988; Darling, 1980; Das, 1970; Griffiths, 1962). So the colonial structure seemed to have survived.

The Superintendent of Police had also to be vigilant about crime, particularly serious crime. All serious criminal cases were treated by the Crime Branch as Special Report Cases. The Superintendent had no connection with non-Special Report Cases, although all First Information Reports were sent to him to keep him informed of the volume of crime. The Superintendent could classify any case as a Special Report Case if he wanted to supervise it. The young IPS recruit was able to learn that crime was not the principal priority for top police executives. They were more concerned with matters of a political nature, collection of intelligence, administrative functions, public relations, and largely, public order policing, i.e., policing of demonstrations, marches. Protests, riots and similar events threatened the public peace (4).

Numerous forms of public discontent were matters of such great concern that they often kept District Superintendents away from their regular schedule. To gain experience in managing disorders and conflicts was considered more important than anything else for the IPS officer on field training. Agitations can take place over any issue, and young people and students are at the forefront of them all (Das, 1983; Bayley, 1969). During the field training of the observer author, he was asked to observe how special police vigilance was required during Muslim festival like *Id* when Hindus were sure to riot if Muslims would sacrifice 'sacred cows'. When the observer author was patrolling with local police during one *Id* festival, they came across an agitating group of Hindus outraged by the sacrifice of a cow in a Muslim neighborhood. The Inspector in charge of the police team ordered the enraged Hindus to disperse as they were menacing to create a disturbance, but they did not pay heed to his orders. The Inspector's face became crimson and flushed, and he with his team following him charged into the crowd with batons and sticks. He was a heavy man with a very large stomach, but the anger caused by the crowd's refusal to follow his orders provided him with the energy to pursue the agitators with furious gusto.

The General Branch handled matters concerning personnel, uniforms, rations, and stationery. It handled inspection reports of all units. Other administrative work included police reports on gun applications, processing of petitions for public meetings, demonstrations, marches and so on, management of the annual budget including travel allowances, and the payment of salaries. This work was carried out by civilian Clerks or *Babus* as they were known in the British days. They were the people who did, what Flack (Quoted by Hunt and Harrison, 1980) describes as "the main donkey-work of the administration."

An important aspect of learning for the IPS trainee is to accompany the Superintendent of Police on his tours of inspection of police stations (5). Once a year, the superintendent of Police inspects each police station to personally assess the quality of the work done by the officer in-charge and his subordinates. The Superintendent's inspections cover crime prevention and detection, discipline, maintenance of station property, and public relations. It is believed that the Superintendent must be clever and thorough during inspections in order to detect the weaknesses in the administration of police stations. Annual inspections were the means used by British Superintendents of Police to make sure of police discipline and productivity in outlying areas of the jurisdiction. They used elephants, horses, and bullock carts to reach many stations. They carried tents for sleeping overnight and lived in bungalows, if available, maintained at government expense for officers on tour. Hunts and Harrison (1980) mention that "the process of inspection was not confined to form an inspection of records and stock-taking of office files." Inspections encouraged "the accessibility of all touring officers ... provided many bits of the jigsaw otherwise missing from the records." The inspections are useful within the context of Indian administrative culture and physical conditions. De (1979) writes:

> The higher officers toured extensively throughout their
> jurisdiction, met people, inspected offices, estimated the efficiency
> of their subordinates and gave direction and guidance, whenever
> necessary.

The job of the police superintendent involved everything that was connected with policing. To the observer author it seemed that there was little time to reflect and think on the part of the chief. It seemed as though there was an unconscious conspiracy to bring everything to the attention of the boss inundating him with petty details of everyday work (Bennis, 1976). Internally, district police administration was totally dominated by the Superintendent of Police who made almost every decision at his police headquarters. Although the District Magistrate and the Superintendent were apparently friendly to each other, the latter resented that the former could intervene in his work. The District Magistrate could stop at a wayside police station, for example and give instructions to the police officials there without the Superintendent's knowledge. Sometimes, the public would go to the District Magistrate with a complaint against the police. Complaints were referred to the Superintendent for inquiry and report to the District Magistrate. The Superintendent of Police resented these referrals.

Diversified career of an IPS officer, the consummate generalist

An IPS officer is expected to be a generalist, an all-rounded police executive able to serve as a leader in all fields of police activities in Armed or Unarmed Branches of the police, at the state or the federal positions of leadership responsibilities. The primary role for which he should be trained is for working as the leader of the police in a district or at a younger age as the head of the police in a subdivision of a district. This is expected to help him get ready for higher leadership positions in policing.

Such young officers should not be sent to armed police battalions because of the very special nature of their operations and the limited scope for an IPS officer to use his trained capacity but upon the completion of district training the observer author was moved to a battalion apparently because there was no career planning by his superiors who were responsible for shaping his career in the best interest of the public. Generally speaking, assignments of higher ranking officers were political and officers were moved for rewarding or punishing them or to utilize them for selfish purposes by political leaders (Hart, 1988; Spangenberg, 1976).

Young IPS officers were also assigned the positions of Subdivisional Police Officers that gave them the first opportunity to them to work as 'real' police executives. The observer author found the position ideal for a young Indian police leader. A subdivisional police officer is free from paper work; all paper work was done at the office of the District Superintendent of Police (see Job training above). In this new position the young officer was able to meet the members of the public and discuss problems of crime and disorder with them. Every police station in the subdivision had the assistance of Village Defense Party, a party of local rural people, who helped police personnel to patrol, investigate, and maintain order. This position without bureaucratic official work provided the young police executive an opportunity to inspire his subordinates to practice value-oriented management (Peters and Waterman, 1982) to work with people, and develop community policing through consultation with the community and learning about the problems people were facing. The position offered a healthy alternative to "the military models of policing" (Das, 1986).

An IPS officer soon moves to the next higher position: the Additional Superintendent of Police from either the position of Assistant Commandant or Subdivisional Police Officer. The observer author was also promoted to that rank and he recalled being totally engaged in quelling public agitations. This is also the period that the selected officers were taken to the Intelligence Bureau, the premier intelligence agency of the country operated by the national government. Those officers who do well at the final examination of the IPS training school are earmarked, selected as core officers as called now, by the Intelligence Bureau (6) to work there. It had happened to the observer author. However, one can return and often returns to the state where one is allocated to. The observer author returned to his state after serving five years in the Intelligence Bureau of the

Government of India in New Delhi.

The most important assignment for an IPS officer is his position as the District Superintendent of Police (7). This is where his training, mental capacity, physical endurance and diplomatic skills are tested to the full. A district superintendent of police is the chief of police or a chief constable. As described in the section on "On the Job Training", district policing is the full service model of policing: management of personnel, providing leadership, handling protests, riots and public disturbances, collecting intelligence, hobnobbing with politicians and keeping political bosses happy, supervising crime investigations, performing as the spokesperson of the police and solving numerous other problems in a large jurisdiction with an enormous population and multitudes of problems which abound in India, the world's most populous democracy with one of the longest history of British colonialism and abysmal depths of poverty.

An IPS officer will move ahead occupying positions of higher rank till he retires. A majority of them retire as Directors General of Police in the states they are allocated to or the heads of federal police agencies. However, the district superintendent's position is the challenging assignment in the career of an IPS officer, the stepping stone for greater responsibilities.

Challenges of policing India and the IPS

This account of the important aspects of education, training, role and status of the IPS officers is intended to convey that these officers are in a unique position to contribute to the better policing in their country. However, there seems to be a lack of focus in training as well as actual work assignments in regard to their role in the appreciation of the challenges. What are those challenges that the IPS officers need to be made aware right from the beginning?

India appeared to be ungovernable (Bayley, 1991). The challenge of ungovernability has posed an insurmountable predicament to the Indian police. They must police a country of one billion inhabitants with a large percentage of the population living in poverty. The country has a history of religious upheavals, political dissensions, and a serious concern with terrorism. The position of the police is very difficult "because if they come into conflict with the mob and control it with efficiency, they are criticized for using violence against harmless citizens. Through excess of caution, they fail to nip rioting in the bud. They are blamed for inefficiency and indifferences" (Shah, 1992: 271). Das (1994: 228) observes:

> Popular cooperation and goodwill is almost nonexistent. The bulk of the police force, the constables, are inadequately educated, badly trained, insufficiently paid, and largely deployed as menial workers. Traditional police work such as preventive patrol, crime prevention, and criminal investigation has been completely neglected because of unrest and disturbances that the police must constantly tackle. Almost all extra resources have been expanded in recent years in building military-like prowess of the police to save the country from chaos. But this is contrary to what the police role should be: a humble functionary working the beat as a helper, friend, and counsel.

The response to chaos, anarchy and disruptive activities has been dependence of the government upon the armed forces like police battalions in the states, the Central Reserve Police, the Border Security Force and other armed units (Das and Verma, 1999). This is crisis policing. There is no doubt that IPS officers as leaders should be able to convince the nation that this trend must stop. Instead, an attempt could be made to increase the strength and capability of the unarmed and civilian police. The IPS leaders should recognize that intelligence apparatus. Intelligence unit from the district administration to the national level is fraught with the potential for abuse. It seemed unnecessary in a democratic but poor country to invest scarce resources in purely traditional police tools: armed strength and secret intelligence.

The colonial tradition of using police as the strong arm of the government has encouraged militarism to thrive, which the IPS leaders must consider as

27

another great challenge. As mentioned above, police autonomy at all levels was one of the most urgent needs. The IPS is dominated by another service in all aspects of the administration. Even in law the police are a suspect institution. Subordinate police officers, particularly the constables, were not utilized for solving problems. Ironically, according to law, the lowest ranking police officers had the same legal powers as their superiors. Nevertheless, there has been no attempt to develop subordinates' personalities, confidence and attitude as seen in such practices as orderlies and the life in the police reserve described elsewhere. The way Constables were treated was immoral, a negation of their human worth and a waste of the nation's public resources (Kumar, 1980). Police organizations in all countries are criticized for adhering to the classical model of management, but in India it was exploitative. This negation of the human worth of subordinates had enormously contributed to the incapacity of the police to safeguard the moral imperatives of a democracy. The absence of organizational democracy and its painful consequences had been captured in agonizing details by Indian and foreign observers of Indian police (Brass, 1990; Hart, 1988; Jeffrey, 1986; Misra, 1986; Rao, 1983; Sinha, 1977).

The colonial tradition of militarism, denial of the organizational democracy and other consequences of authoritarianism are aggravated by the politics of scarcity, which encompass such challenges as extremely limited chances of promotion, scarce emoluments, undesirable working conditions, and similar other consequences associated with a non-affluent society. (For example, the police in general can not be provided with automobiles, and most patrols are necessarily on foot and bicycles, which are the common method of movement). Although corruption is not necessarily a product of the lack of material well being (Das, forthcoming), it bedevils Indian police enormously. The police are known as corrupt, but it may not be the most daunting challenge of the Indian police as experienced by the observer author. He heard that some officers were bribable, but generally they did not neglect their public duty. The issue of corruption is realistically presented by Bayley (1966) as follows:

> The corrupt are not always unable; nor are they always unpatriotic. These propositions seem especially true of underdeveloped countries where the rewards for government service are so piteously low. Where corruption is often necessary to provide basic necessities of life to oneself and one's family, it becomes a necessary means of ensuring a supply of able and willing public servants. Furthermore, in developing nations it is an indispensable means of reconciling insufficient wage rates with the claims of traditional society operating through extended family and clan ties. The civil servant cannot wish away these obligations. Through corruption he taxes society with preserving an important element of social continuity.

There have been serious charges of police corruption and brutality claimed against the Indian Police. Raghavan claims that media complaints along with court decisions leave the impression that the police lack integrity (1994: 227). Police brutality may be a more serious problem, according to Raghavan, than corruption. The basis for this claim is the number of deaths that occur each year to individuals under police custody. The history of police misconduct has extensively been reported by the news media over the last several decades (228-229). One Indian author (Vadackumchery, 2000) even questions if it is a myth to talk of a human rights friendly police in India. Lobo (1993) believes that acts of police violence can be related to the public's views of the police. When the public holds the police in low regard this can contribute to more acts of violence by the police. The uncontrollable use of force decreases the respect the public will show towards the police. Higher incidents of police violence occur in countries where the police are not highly regarded by the public (1993: 30). Behavioral modification of the Indian police is the focus of attention of Vadackumchery's *Policing the Largest Democracy: 50 Years and After* (1998).

Mathur (1994) in his book on the *Indian Police* discusses the manifestation of marginal crimes in Indian police work. Usually, marginal crimes begin with small irregularities such as presenting false evidence to obtain a

29

conviction. According to Mathur, the following are a list of well know manifestations of marginal crimes committed by Indian police officers. They are (76-77):

1. Concealment of crime by burking and minimization of offenses at the time of registration.
2. Fabrication of false evidence and confinement of suspects beyond authorized time limit.
3. Illegal detention and wrongful confinements of suspects beyond authorized time limit.
4. Criminal assault, rape, and death cases in police custody.
5. Deaths in 'Police encounters' with criminals and dacoits.
6. Use of excessive force and third degree methods of interrogation resulting in grievous hurt and injuries.
7. Illegal activities including strikes by police unions.
8. Submission of final reports in actual crimes for various other considerations.
9. Brutality, rudeness and abrasive behavior and ill-treatment of weaker sections of the society particularly economically poorer people.
10. Corruption and illegal gratification in police working.
11. Failure to take effective steps against gambling, smuggling, drinking, prostitution and other offenses for extraneous considerations.
12. Total indifference and connivance to white collar crime and socio-economic offenses and failure to effectively curb such criminal offenses in their respective jurisdictions.
13. Endemic police lying in police operation

Apart from the unique consequences the police suffer as a result of the cultural, social, legal and psychological aspects of the Indian environment and conditions (Vadackumchery, 2001, the police in India, including the IPS members, are more than likely to be victims of universal negative consequences

30

of policing. Did the IPS attract only those who were attracted to policing in the USA, for example? As a profession the police may attract certain kinds of people (Alpert and Dunham, 1992; McNamara, 1967) with characteristics like conservatism and authoritarianism. Coercion which "sets off policemen from society" (Brown, 1981) also made the IPS officers feel isolated as the observer author experienced. They were aware of "the capacity to use force" (Bittner, 1980). They must be "suspicious" (Skolnick, 1967) of "symbolic assailants" which made police defensive and distrustful of the people they do not know well. The IPS officers could not have been free from "the pressures" a police officer "feels to prove himself efficient" which are not "unlike those felt by an industrial worker." The IPS officers might not be sensitive to "the practical dilemma faced by the police required to maintain order under a democratic rule of law" as it happens to the police in other countries.

Does training at the police school socialize the IPS officers to police culture? The answer can be guessed on the basis of what happens to the police trainee in the USA. Manning and Van Maanen (1978) refer to the academy period in an American police recruit's life as the time when the process of "individualism possessed by a recruit is to be minimized in favor of the collective front." They add that the academy "may, in fact forcefully and consequentially help to shape the patrolman's working personality." Some values that police training presented as valuable were obedience, conformity, toughness, outward appearance, and physical discipline. At the training school the IPS recruit learned that outward appearance was to be so important that when they came to the districts they, like the observer author, were likely to try to impress all police personnel with the same philosophy. Were physical appearance, smartness, and military discipline necessary for practical police work? Notwithstanding the fact that these are not perhaps the crucial qualifications of a good police officer, values assimilated at training made the police officer associate "the physical image" with "the moral image" (Harris, 1978). Police trainees learned that a person who

31

"shaved each day, kept his hair short, shined his shoes regularly, and wore pressed clothes could be expected to be a law abiding, and a moral person." Conversely, "those persons who grew beards, wore their hair long, and wore unkempt clothes … could be expected to connote something less than moral." The feeling of being "pariahs" (Brown, 1981; Wilson, 1963; Banton, 1964) was something that was part of IPS officers at the Foundational Course, and in the districts. Many IPS officers would not display such feelings publicly. They keep up an appearance particularly before their personnel because "how subordinates view their leaders is important in police agency, for it has a major influence upon morale" (Goldstein, 1986). These are remarks the observer can make on the basis of the collective experience of his colleagues and himself.

Forging a vision for the future

If the future of the Indian police is to be better than the past and the present, steps must be taken that will help making the police contribute more significantly to safety, security and quality of life in the country. In this task the IPS officers should play a significant role as police leaders. They may think of some simple, basic and workable strategies like the following:

Community policing is one strategy that could be used by the Indian Police to enhance their cooperation with their fellow countrymen. The police in Bhiwandi (State of Maharashtra) have made an attempt to establish community policing. This community known for its Hindu-Muslim conflicts formed a committee of thirty members from each religious sect to meet once a week to discuss various issues with the local Sub-Inspector of Police. The police not only assist the community in police matters but also in non-police matters such as the supply of electricity, and the availability of rationed food commodities. The police have developed a close relationship with the people in the community and the monitoring of Hindi-Muslim relations does not require much effort on the part of the police. Because of the police involvement the violent actions between

Hindus and Muslims occur very infrequently (Raghavavan, 1999: 168). This example shows that the Indian Police can obtain the cooperation of the public with policing strategies such as community policing. This will also make the police sensitive to the people composed of diversity in religion, language, culture and economic status (Meliala. 2001).

There are several factors in the Indian situation that will prove congenial to practice of community policing.

In spite of an inherited negative attitude, the public seemed ready, as experienced by the observer author, to accept well-meaning, public-spirited individual officers as friends. When the observer author was District Superintendent of Police he noted that the members of the public, those from the rural as well as urban areas, were willing to work with the police. The rural folks in the State of Assam, for example, cooperated with the police taking part in the work of the Village Defense Party which consisted of volunteers who took part in citizen patrols under police supervision. Since the Indian public was used to being treated harshly and exploitatively by officialdom, they appeared to be pleasantly surprised with even small gestures of bureaucratic sympathy and respectful treatment. The police were found all over the vast country including in the areas where there were no other governmental agencies and they could literally serve the people philosophers, friends and guides. Accessibility, a problem in motorized patrol operations, was absent everywhere except the large cities as the police mostly walked or used bicycles. The majority of the subordinate police officers came from rural areas and modest economic background. Thus, the existing police characteristics, the nature of the Indian people, and the police methods of operations provided them with excellent opportunities to work with the public. Indian police enjoyed the infrastructure for community, problem-oriented policing.

Another strategy that could improve the Indian Police relations (7) with the public is increasing the numbers of women police. Women officers can perform a wide variety of functions. In addition to dealing with women crime victims, they can also deal with women in public demonstrations, which disrupt vehicular traffic and threaten public peace. Several states have established all-women stations (Raghavavan, 1999). Women are playing a larger role in police agencies throughout the world and the Indian Police have numerous examples of how police agencies use women in their various operations. It has been commented (Bhardwaj, 1999) that fortunately there are no distinctions between male and female officers in regard to salary, medical facilities, travel facilities, workplace rules, and others. However, women police are employed at lower subordinate ranks than their male counterparts, and women officers, particularly those of lower rank, believe that they are much less accepted and recognized. Bhardwaj also notes that the profession has responded to the changing role of women in society. It should be noted that if discrimination is to be eliminated against women than they should have the same opportunities as their male counterparts. Women should be given the opportunity to develop the respect, trust, confidence and cooperation of the public for the police.

It should be realized that a more humane, effective and purposeful use must be made of subordinate officers with modification of the rigid organizational hierarchy which smacks of the Indian caste system and of course the colonial administrative culture. The central and state governments had no way of motivating subordinate officers like constables to take the IPS and the State Civil Service Examinations so that they could look forward to career advancement. For ethnic groups in India there are special concessions for entry into the All-India Services. Special provisions could be made for police candidates and serving police officers. The practice of community policing in India will enhance the job satisfaction of subordinate officers as it calls for delegation and high trust in subordinates (Stevens, 2001). Police reorganization to replace the military model has been suggested as a remedy of high stress in subordinates (Mathur, 1999). There was the need for re-thinking of the relationship between the colleagues in the IAS and the IPS. The colonial tradition and methods of operations, with the District Magistrates as little Viceroys, should be eliminated. The police are to prevent and detect crime, but they must also serve the society in every possible way. The IPS officers should be fully committed to the mission of providing leadership to the police, inspiring their personnel, and drawing strength from the people. There does not seem to be a continuing preoccupation with reforming the leadership of the Indian police which the IPS members can do through the IPS Association.

With two hundred years of colonialism, it is natural that the public image of the police was poor. Historically, the police had inherited from the British days a reputation of being the ruler's stooges. It has been observed (Shekhar, 1999) that the current system which has perpetuated the legacy of the colonialism by permitting the practice of sharing the spoils at the expense of the common citizens is acceptable to the political leaders and the bureaucracy. Shekhar advocates a paradigm shift citing the recommendation of the National Police Commission (1977-81). In this process the change agents are naturally the members of the IPS. It is to be pointed out the IPS Association never took a public stand against the immoral practices of politicians, never advocated building a tradition of being peoples' police, and calling upon the fellow members as police leaders for change. The IPS Association must show moral aggressiveness to defend correct practices based on principles. The Association could provide benefits to officers who became victims of unfair political manipulations. It has also been suggested that the new paradigm mentioned above should include the restructuring the Indian police within the framework of the constitution and Fundamental Rights instead of the Police Act of 1861 which created the colonial police.

In brief, changes in the Indian police will take place with assumption of the legitimate role of the IPS as change leaders. The strategies for change should ensure the utilization of the people as partners of the police and making it possible for the subordinate police officials to contribute their full share in shaping the police as an instrument of public service.

Endnotes

(1) State governments in India are responsible for hiring police personnel who can enter the service generally at three levels: Constable, Assistant Sub-Inspector/Sub-Inspector, and Deputy Superintendent. The first three ranks are called non-gazetted; the last one is a gazetted position. Transfers, promotions, and other service particulars of a gazetted officer are published in the *State Gazette,* a periodic publication that contains information about all major activities undertaken by the government. Similar matters concerning non-gazetted officers, the subordinate ranks are not announced at the level of the state government but by each local police district. The gazetted and the non-gazetted ranks differ in terms of salary, fringe benefits, power and prestige.

Deputy Superintendent is the only gazetted rank among the officers hired by the State Government. Although Indian terms—*Sipahi* for Constable and *Darogha* for Sub-Inspector—existed in pre-British days, no equivalent term exists in native languages for Deputy Superintendent. The rank was a British invention and the colonial administration wanted local people in the middle echelons of the bureaucracy to ' act as go-betweens for the top English-speaking British administrators and for the native functionaries engaged in lower level responsibilities. Deputy Superintendents were middle managers who were created on the recommendation of the Indian Police Commission in 1902-1903. Today top commanders of the Indian Police Service may come from any part of the country with little knowledge of the local language, customs, and manners. Deputy Superintendents are also useful for them. The states of the Indian Union hire Deputy Superintendents of Police through the State Public Service Commissions, semi-autonomous agencies, as per provisions of the Indian

Constitution. Between the ranks of Deputy Superintendent and Sub-Inspector there is the rank of Inspector, which is attained only through promotions. An Inspector is regarded as a semi-gazetted rank with better salary, more privileges and higher powers than other ranks but is less regarded compared to the gazetted ranks.

The Indian Police Service recruit joins the service as an Assistant Superintendent. This is the lowest and first rank of the police command hierarchy, followed by Superintendent, Deputy Inspector General, Inspector General, and Director General. An Assistant Superintendent is the result of direct recruitment; all the higher ranks are filled by promotions. A Deputy Superintendent, the highest directly recruited rank in the State Police, can be promoted to all the senior ranks to which an IPS officer may aspire. However, he must be officially promoted to the Indian Police Service before he can occupy any rank above Superintendent of Police. This promotion is based on seniority and on merit.

(2) States in India have another armed branch of the police: the Armed Police Battalions. They are India's gendarmerie, but unlike the French *Gendarmerie*, the Canadian Royal Mounted Police, the Alaskan State Troopers, the Italian *Carrabinieri*, or the Spanish *Guardia Civil*, the police battalions in India are not engaged in regular police work. They are used for emergencies, controlling state borders, and special police operations. They are also placed at the disposal of a District Superintendent of Police who may only use them in his special operations. Since 1861 when the Indian Police Act was introduced, policing in India is performed by civilian police officers, not by military officers (Brogden, 1987; Stead, 1985; Jeffries, 1952).

A police battalion is headed by a Commandant with the rank of Superintendent of Police and can be either from the IPS or the State Police Service. Below the Commandant are a Second-in-Command who is an Additional Superintendent and five or six Company Commanders who are either Deputy

Superintendents or Assistant Superintendents of Police. These battalions are engaged in border disputes among states, for preventing depredations by armed marauders across state or international borders, and in controlling massive riots which cannot be handled by a district's armed or unarmed police. These battalions may be sent to reinforce district police, or they can be given independent tasks.

The armed police battalion to which the observer author was assigned was given the task of fighting against armed depredations of one ethnic group who were engaged in political struggles. They were the Nagas, an Indian tribe who were fighting for a country of their own and were attacking villages in the bordering Assam in the furtherance of their demand. During the British Raj they had a district within the State of Assam called the Naga Hill District. After India's Independence they began agitating for their own independence. The Naga demand for independence became so violent and determined that the Government of India created a new state called Nagaland in order to appease them and keep them within the country. When the observer author was an Assistant Commander, the Nagas had not yet been given a state of their own. Attacks on the villages in Assam bordering their district were serious.

The observer author was the head of another police battalion which was deployed at the Assam-Arunachal border. One of the newest states in India, it was created in deference to public agitation which resulted in the creation of seven different states out of what had been Assam. Many disputes occur among the states including disputes over borders and over depleting natural wealth like forests, water, and other resources. The Second Assam Police Battalion guarded the territory of Assam against intrusions by people in the bordering state of Arunachal Pradesh. They operated border patrols, checked the movements of vehicles across state borders, and collected intelligence regarding the activities of the battalions in Arunachal Pradesh. Although the lack of Indianness, national cohesion, and unity is due to many historical and contemporary problems, the rivalry between different regions of India seems to be wholly caused by the politics of scarcity (Weiner, 1962).

This battalion also provided armed support to the local Superintendent of Police. The battalion personnel were utilized for all operations that, in his opinion, could not be handled by his District Armed Police and police station personnel. These operations included demonstrations, labor disputes, riots, and serious crimes. In the battalions, all subordinate ranks were responsible for the physical maintenance of the compound. Civilian police personnel, non-armed police Constables and other ranks are generally exempted from physical labor in police stations because not much emphasis is placed on keeping these stations clean. However, these ranks can also be asked to do manual work, because no budgetary provisions are made for the maintenance of station grounds and buildings. Since the British *Raj,* the police in India have always had fatigue duty or *Kamjhari.* Since the Second Assam Police Battalion was moving to a new location the personnel had to build roads, plant trees, construct parade grounds, and collect building materials from the forests to make its new location a permanent home.

(3) In India, police are armed or unarmed. The Unarmed Branch (UB) police personnel-constables, sub-inspectors etc, work in police stations which are located in a large plot of land with housing for the married personnel and barracks for constables who live without families. The Armed Branch (AB) personnel are housed in the District Police Reserves. They are assigned to static security posts in front of the houses of ministers and other important public officials, senior police officers including the Superintendent of Police, the district Magistrate, and to guard other vulnerable places. They also provide security to visiting state and federal government dignitaries including Ministers. They may work as office orderlies. Gazetted offices are allowed to keep them as orderlies at home, a practice that is badly abused. The Indian Police Service (IPS) officers feel privileged that they have orderlies, because their counterparts in the Indian Administrative Service (lAS) do not have them. Many Constables do not like to work as orderlies in the homes of officers, but they have no choice in the matter.

The Police Reserve houses many disgruntled people with important reasons for their lack of morale: poor housing, dull work, and inadequate salary. Armed constables must also line up in proper formations, must be present at roll calls, must march in parades, do physical training, and perform tiresome duties. They are expected to remain alert night and day to respond to emergencies. Delinquent ranks, particularly Constables, can be given summary punishment by a gazetted officer in the district. They appear in the orderly room before a presiding officer. Subordinates can also appear before such an officer if they have grievances about any matter at work or at home. Confinement cells called "Quarter Guards" are maintained at Police Reserves where a constable can be kept confined up to fifteen days. The Police Reserve contained a reserve office, a district armory, a clothing store and a small hospital or a clinic. The establishment was headed by a Sub-Inspector or an Inspector, known as the Reserve Officer. Unless the Superintendent of Police was particularly attentive and careful, District Police Reserves could become a place for illicit drinking, gambling, or narcotics trading. These activities were likely to occur in a place housing a large group of rather poorly educated and poorly paid people living together in uncomfortable conditions without recreational facilities.

(4) A demonstration can be organized over a supposedly unfair university examination or an unpopular taxation proposal by the government (Bayley, 1969; Das, 1983). In India the issues causing public agitations vary from state to state. The people participating in agitations are mostly students, helped financially by opposition politicians eager to embarrass the government. In the State of Assam the Bengalis who migrated from former East Pakistan (presently, Bangaldesh) caused widespread student disturbances. The Assamese, the original inhabitants of the state, have historically resented the presence of the Bengalis from East Bengal which was part of the Bengal province under the British *Raj* (before it became part of Pakistan following the British departure from India). Migrants are viewed in Assam as an economic and cultural threat (Weiner, 1975). Agitation

erupted in the universities in Assam from time to time against Bengali students. As District Superintendent of Police the observer author handled riots at a local university over the issue of Bengali students.

When the observer author was promoted as Additional Superintendent of Police, although conventionally this position was mainly used to supervise Special Report Cases, he came to be involved in primarily handling riots. The local people were aggressively agitating for the location of a public oil refinery in Assam to refine its new found crude oil. The Government of India wanted the refinery in the state of Bihar, but people in Assam demanded that it be installed in their state. Handling protests was left to every commander's discretion, and they received no written instructions on how they should be subdued. The Government wanted to avoid political embarrassment, and usually handling public disturbances involved keeping patient watch over the agitators to see that they did not break the law. When they broke laws, the police could intervene to physically stop violence by dispersing the crowds and arresting leaders. The police did not need to understand the causes of the disturbances. Certain measures to prevent violence and demonstrations were taken politically. Sometimes the District Magistrates would take the initiative by having dialogues with the leaders of public agitations. Only infrequently would the police undertake consultations with the agitators before an actual demonstration, although energetic Superintendents might. Generally, the police reacted to all agitations as passive agents.

(5) As a young Indian police officer the observer author read with a romantic fervor, nostalgia, and sense of history the inspection notes of the British superintendents. They were generally very methodical and meticulous in recording their inspection notes in long hand but they were also somewhat eccentric. In a very remote police station the observer author came across an inspection note by a British superintendent from the colonial period. He expressed a sense of outrage that the *Darogha,* the official in charge of the police station,

was felling large trees in the station compound for firewood. The British Chief threatened the *Daroga* with dire consequences if one more tree was cut without his written permission. In another inspection note it was mentioned that the official at the head of the station was not allowing a subordinate to pursue his college degree. The official was directed to encourage his subordinate. Many British officers were also extremely careful in accounting for the cash kept at the police station, in inspecting the British government's property, and in taking note of anything of material value.

(5) The Intelligence Bureau in India appeared to be large bureaucracy. As an Assistant Director in the Intelligence Bureau, the observer author was not required to keep in mind the important values and norms of the police in democratic nations, i.e., political neutrality, adherence to the rule of law, and respect for privacy of those who were spied upon Assistant Directors and other top officers produced daily reports that were interesting but did not focus on the national objectives. Intelligence officials appeared to the observer author to have suffered from "an onset of intellectual, institutional, or behavioral stagnation." Because some top leaders were unable to shake off "ideological" and "doctrinaire commitment' (Jeffrey-Jones, 1989), they did a disservice to the development of democracy in India. Bureaucratic endeavors to acquire increasing power and prestige particularly in rivalry with the newly emerging agency for foreign intelligence, the Research and Analysis Wing, (Raina, 1981) were palpable. Secrecy and lack of visibility are powers that allow an intelligence organization to indulge in dictatorial management. Police organizations need to be open, because openness helps them become democratic and accountable to the community. Although "democracy depends upon secret intelligence for its survival, yet the relationship between the two has always been controversial, and, at times, mutually harmful" (Jeffrey-Jones, 1989).

(6) Generally, it took 7 to 10 years for an IPS officer to move to a district as Superintendent of Police. A district would have around 5,000 police personnel

who were deployed in a few Sub-Divisions, some Circles, and several Police Stations. The personnel would belong to the District Armed and Unarmed Branches, and there were some elements of the police battalion. Besides, a considerable number of Home Guards who were young members of the community with nominal training in drills, weapons, physical combat and some security tasks were employed by the District Superintendent of Police. They were kept as a reserve force (they receive an emolument when they work).

Labor disputes, public agitations, protest marches; strikes, and demonstrations which were often accompanied by the violent destruction of property and injuries to people are events that demand considerable attention from the Superintendent. Haphazard traffic without adequate control services always constituted a menace on the streets. On Indian roads the police control motor vehicles, bicycles, cycle rickshaws, bullock carts, elephant and horse carriages, pedestrians, and domestic animals. Road accidents and mishaps were matters of concern for the police leader in the district. Natural disasters like floods can cause thousands of people homeless. Bandits who committed physical violence including rape looted affluent homes in rural areas where police protection was minimal. These crimes, known as *dacoity*, were considered heinous. Local politicians regularly attempt to intervene in day-to-day police work for his augmenting their political goals. Very critical reports in the press usually prompted the state police headquarters to demand explanations from the Superintendent of Police about various unsavory matters usually reported in the press. Thus, there were multifarious problems and challenges for the Superintendent. However, because of a caste hierarchy, the ordinary rank-and-file police officials were not part of the problem solving process. They were basically engaged in carrying out orders. Subordinate police officers were powerless and often felt inadequate because of the centralized nature of the district police administration. They also constantly complained of the lack of proper transportation, weak public support, the manipulations of politicians, and the inadequate time for investigation (detectives are not assigned to the police station, and uniformed police sub-inspectors conduct all investigations at the levels of police stations). Many police personnel in the lower ranks were without the basic amenities of life and lacked social status. They had neither the benefit of hygiene nor the luxury of access to motivators. The morale of the people on the job was not very high. Neither was policing a prestigious occupation. All powers and privileges were concentrated with the chief. Police personnel, poorly paid and belonging to the lower socio-economic classes, tend to view their bosses as superior beings (Austin, 1990). Police personnel also were without a great many rights that the people in the general, too, did not enjoy (Kohli, 1988; Sinha, 1977).

(7) The police suffered from the stigma left from the era of British imperialism when the indigenous police fought against their own freedom fighters and maltreated the public who had traditionally suffered from government highhandedness with equanimity (Arnold, 1985; Smith, 1981). The wide gulf between the police and public during the British rule could be imagined through the following words of a perceptive analyst. About the position of the British Indian government, Morris-Jones (1964) writes:

> Government itself was far away in a capital seldom or never seen and its remoteness only increased its imposing stature; the power and the authority were awesome; it was Government, *Raj, Sarkar.* Yet its little finger was a continuous presence in the alleyways between the huts. Like a great god it had its contrasting aspects, giver and taker of all, protector and tax collector. What was important is that it was respected and that the necessity for its existence and strength was accepted and even perhaps understood.

The Indian police were not 'trusted' by the Indian Evidence Act created by the British. According to the provisions of this statute, confessions before police officers were not admissible as evidence. Police officers could search a home without the presence of two or more respected local people (Lushing, 1982). All these handicaps continue after the British left.

44

References

Alpert, Geoffrey, P. and Roger G. Dunham 1992. *Policing Urban America.* Prospect Heights, Illinois: Waveband Press, Inc.

Arnold, David. 1985. Human Sacrifice and British — Kond Relations, 1759 — 1862. In Anana A. Yang, ed. *Crime and Criminality in British India.* Tucson: The University of Arizona press.

Austin, James E. 1990. *Managing in Developing Countries: Strategic Analysis and Operative Techniques.* New York: The Free Press.

Banton, Michael. 1964. *The Policeman in the Community.* New York: Basic Books.

Bawa, P.S.1999. *An Imperative of rights: A new paradigm for police.* India, New Delhi: Har-Anand.

Das, Dilip, Editor. 1994. *Police Practices: An International Review.* Metuchen, NJ: The Scarecrow Press.

Bayley, David H. 1991 Personal Conversation. San Francisco.

•1969. *The Police and Political Development in India.* Princeton: Princeton University Press.

•1966. The Effects of Corruption in a Developing Nation. *The Western Political Quarterly,* 19 (4), 719-732.

Bennis, Waren. 1976. *Unconscious Conspiracy.* New York: AMACOM.

Bhardwaj, Aruna. 1999. Women in uniform: Emergence of women police in Delhi. India, New Delhi: Regency.

Bittner, Egon. 1980. *The Function of Police in Modern Society.* Cambridge, Massachusetts: Oelgeschlager, Gunn & Ham, Publishers.

Brass, Paul R. 1990. *The New Cambridge History of India.* New York: Cambridge University Press.

Bretcher, Michael. 1969. Political Leadership in India: An Analysis of Elite Attitude. New York: Frederick A. Praeger.

Brogden, Michael E. 1987. The Emergence of the Police: The Colonial Dimension. *British Journal of Criminology* 27 (1), 4-14.

Brown, Michael K. 1981. *Working the Street.* New York: Russell Sage Foundation.

Cohen, Stephen P. 1988. The military and India's Democracy. In Atul Kohli, ed. *India's Democracy.* Princeton: Princeton University Press.

Das, Dilip K. 1986. Military Models of Policing. *Canadian Police College Journal* 10 (4), 267-285.

1985. The Image of American Police in Comparative Literature. *Police Studies* 8 (2), 74-83.

2003. Corruption: A global overview. In Sarre, Rick; Das, Dilip and Albrecht, H.A.J, (eds). Policing Corruption: A global perspective. Lanham, Maryland: Lexington

Das, Dilip K. and Verma, Arvind, Tradition of armed police in Indian police. *Policing: A journal of Police Strategy.*

1983. Student Agitation and Police: A Comparative Study. *Police Studies* 6 (2), 53-63.

Das, Durga. 1970. *India from Curzon to Nehru and After.* New York: The John Day Company.

De, Nitish R. 1979. Bureaucracy: Obsolescence and Innovation. In S. C. Dube, ed. *Public Services and Social Responsibility.* New Delhi: Vikas Publishing House Pvt. Ltd.

Dutt, S. K. 1965. Personal Interview. New Delhi.

Diaz, S.M. 1994. "Police in India," in *Police Practices: An International Review,* D. Das, editor, Metuchen, N.J.: Scarecrow Press.

Goldstein, Herman. 1986. Controlling and Reviewing police — Citizen Contacts. In Thomas Barker and David Carter, eds. *Police Deviance.* Cincinnati: Anderson Publishing company.

Griffiths, Sir. Percival. 1962. *Modern India.* New York: Frederick A. Praeger.
1971. *To Guard My People: The History of the Indian Police.* London: Ernest Benn Ltd.

Halbfass, Wilhelm. 1988. *India and Europe.* Albany: State University of New York Press.

Harris,Richard N. 1973. *The Police Academy: An Inside View.* New York: John Wiley and Sons 1978.

The Police Academy and the Professional Self-Image. In Peter K. Manning and John Van Maanen, eds. *Policing: A View from the Street.* Santa Monica, California: Goodyear Publishing company.

Hart, Henry C. 1988. Political Leadership in India: Dimensions and Limits. In Abul Kohli, ed. *(India's Democracy: An Analysis of Changing State — Society Relations.* Princeton: Princeton University Press.

Hunt, Roland and John Harrison. 1980. *The District Officer in India. 1930 – 1947.* London: Scholar Press.

Jeffrey, Robin. 1986. *What's Happening to India?* New York: Holmes & Meir.

Jeffrey-Jones, Rhodri. 1989. *The CIA and America and Democracy.* New Haven: Yale University Press.

Jeffries, Sir Charles. 1952. *The Colonial Police.* London: Max Parrish.

Kohli, Atul. 1988. *India's Democracy.* Princeton: Princeton University Press.

Kumar, Anand. 1989. *State and Society in India.* New Delhi: Radiant Publishers.

Lobo, John. 1993. "The Police and the Community: Some Areas of Concern," in *Police and Community,* R.C. Dikshit and G. Rajshah, editors, Trishul Publications.

Lushing, Susan C. 1982. Comparative Criminal Justice - Search and Seizure, Interrogation, and Identification of Suspect in India: A Research Note. *Journal of Criminal Justice* 10 (3), 239-245.

Mathur, Krishna Mohan. 1994. *Indian Police: Role and Challenges,* New Delhi, India: Gyan Publishing Hourse.

McNamara, John. 1967. Uncertainties of Police Work: The Relevance of Police Recruits' Backgrounds and Training. In David J. Bordua, ed. *The Police: Six sociological Essays.* New York: John Wiley and sons.

47

Manning, Peter K. and John Van Maanen, 1978. Socialization for Policing. In Peter K. Manning and John Van Maanen, eds. *Policing: A View from the Street*. Santa Monica: Goodyear Publishing Company.

Meliala, Adrianus. The notion of sensitivity in policing, *International Journal of Sociology of Law*, 29 (2), 99-111.

Misra, Shailendra. 1986. *Police Brutality: An Analysis of Police Behaviour*. New Delhi: Vikas Publishing House Pvt Ltd.

Morris-Jones, W. H. 1964. *The Government and Politics of India*. London: Hutchinsons & Co.

Peters, Thomas J. and Robert H. Waterman, Jr. 1982. *In Search of Excellence: Lessons from America's Bet Run Companies*. New York: Harper & Row.

Radelet, Louis A. 1986. *The Police and the Community*. New York: Macmillan.

Raghavan, R.K. 1999. *Policing A Democracy: A Comparative Study of India and the US*. New Delhi, India: Manohar Publishers.

Raj Gopal. 2001. Personal conversation. India, Hyderabad.

Raina,Asoka. 1981. *Inside RAW: The Story of India's Secret Service*. New Delhi: Vikas Publishing House Pvt Ltd.

Rao, S. Venugopal. 1983. *Crime in our Society: A Political Prospective*. New Delhi: Vikas Publishing House Pvt Ltd.

Shah, Giriraj. 1992. *The Indian Police: A Retrospect*. New Delhi, India: Himalaya Publishing House.

Shekhar, Rajendra.1999. *Not a licence to kill: Police needs paradigm-shift*. India, Delhi: Konark.

Sinha, Sachidanad. 1977. *Emergency in Perspective: Reprieve and Challenge*. New Delhi: Heritage Publishers.

Skolnick, Jerome H. 1967. *Justice without Trial: Law Enforcement in a Democratic Society*. New York: John Wiley and Sons.

Smith, Vincent A. 1981. *The Oxford History of India*. Delhi: Oxford University Press.

Spangenberg, Bradford. 1976. *British Bureaucracy in India: Status, Policy and the I.C.S. in the Late* 19th *Century*. Columbia, Missouri: South Asia Books.

Stead, Philip John. 1985. *The Police of Britain*. New York: MacMillan.

Stevens, Dennis J. 2001. Community Policing and Managerial Technique: Total Quality Management Techniques. *Police Journal*, 74 (1), 26-41.

Van Maanen, John. 1978. Kinsmen in Repose: Occupational Perspectives of Patrolmen. In Peter K. Manning and John Van Maanen, eds. *Policing: A View from the Street*. Santa Monica, California: Goodyear Publishing Company, Inc.

Vadackumchery, James. 1999. *Third Millennium police: Take off trends in India*. India, New Delhi: A.P.H. Publishing. 2000. *Human Rights Friendly Police: A myth or reality India*, New Delhi: A.P.H. Publishing.

1998 *Policing the largest democracy: 50 years and after*. India, New Delhi: A.P. H. Publishing.

1998. *Indian Police-2001: What went wrong here?* India, New Delhi: A.P.H. Publishing.

Verma, Arvind. 1999. "Cultural Roots of Police Corruption in India," *Policing: An International Journal of Police Strategies and Management*, Volume 22, No. 3, 264-279.

Waldman, Amy. Surplus of Food and Starvation. *The New York Times*. December 2, 2002, P A3).

Weiner, Myron. 1962. *The Politics of Scarcity*. Chicago: University of Chicago press.

1975 *When Migrants Succeed and Natives Fall: Assam and its Migrants*. Cambridge, Massachusetts: Centre for International Studies, M.I.T.

Wilson, James Q. 1963. The Police and their Dilemma: A Theory. *Public Policy* 186-2 16.

Wolpert, Stanley, 1982. *A New History of India*. New York; Oxford University Press.

* Sincere gratitude is due to K. S. Dhillon (IPS, retired), Deepak Dutt (IPS, Additional Director General of Police (Assam, India), S. Subramanian (IPS, retired) and Arvind Verma (IPS, now a faculty member at Indiana University, Bloomington, USA) for their careful review of the manuscript and suggestions.
Policing in Canada, India, Germany, Australia,

Chapter 2

Politics, Morale, and Respectability

The Australian and New Zealand Police

Introduction

The observer author visited New Zealand immediately after his study of the police in Australia. The impressions of the police in both countries gathered through observation were almost inseparable in his mind. It also appeared to the observer author that the Australian and the New Zealand police were strikingly different and it is this contrast that made it tempting to combine these two different police in one chapter. For the reflection and analysis on the themes of politics and the police, and on the factors including politics that affect police morale and respectability, the observer author found that these two police entities provided a fascinating comparative study with their wide array of difference in organization and environment.

While this is one of the reasons why this chapter presents the police of two countries together, one must also bear in mind that the police in Australia and New Zealand have several elements in common: they are former British colonies, English speaking countries with deep-rooted connections to England and they are members of the British Commonwealth.

There are also lighter reasons derived mainly from the fact that the observer author's visit happened to be during the football season. He experienced at firsthand that the Australians and the New Zealanders have a friendly rivalry, particularly in sports. During that football season the observer author noted Wellington patrol officers were mustering in front of the television set in the social area at the Central Police Station when there was a football match between Australia and New Zealand. Streets were without police cars because the police knew that the general public was so intense with interest in the match between Australia and New Zealand that not a single soul was likely to be far from a television set and so the streets were safe. The scenes at the police stations, the enthusiasm of the police officers cheering for New Zealand and the empty streets in Wellington during the final match between these two countries were fresh in observer author's mind goading him to synthesize the notes on the police of the two friendly rivals.

Finally, it is necessary to discuss the limitations of the study right at the outset. It must be noted here that the observer author did not begin his observation and study of the police in Australia and New Zealand with the objective of exploring the differences in the degrees of political involvement, morale, and respectability of the police in these two different countries. The themes chosen in this chapter emerged during the study through participation in police patrols, observation of police work on the streets, police stations and in homes as well as other places which the police visited, accompanied by the observer author, in response to calls or complaints. The revelations, the discovery, about the negative consequences of politics in the police and the related issues occurred during the course of observation in Australia which the observer author brought with him as he began the study in New Zealand. It is to be stated further that these observations were made almost fifteen years back and to that extent they are severely outdated. However, the analysis and explanations made on the basis of the field observations made years back have been updated by the study of the contemporary literature. Besides, authors have had the benefit of a critical evaluation of this chapter, particularly in regard to the applicability to the present situation, by police scholars from Australia and New Zealand like Rick Sarre, Tim Prenzler, and Greg Newbold. In view of these developments, the authors feel confident that the validity of the original analysis is intact. Moreover, the field

52

observation took place in State of Victoria in Australia and Wellington and its surrounding areas in New Zealand. But these observations have been generalized to the police in the countries again on the basis of the comparative evaluation of the local observations with the Australian and New Zealand police literature relating to the police in general in both countries.

Historical, political, and cultural contexts

In area, Australia is almost as large as the United States. With 40 percent of the land within the tropics, the populated areas are within the temperate regions. European colonialists who came to this continent in the eighteenth century were "predominantly English-Scottish-Irish-Welsh in origin" (Tumbull, 1966). Its colonization by England in 1788 was "merely a shift to dispose of the superfluity of criminals, who could no longer be sent to the American colonies." Australia became a receiving ground for an English society "troubled by these by-products of a society in flux." By 1868 "dumping of England's felons in Australia" ended as "ignobly, as it had begun." After the gold rush ended in 1885, Melbourne with its natural harbor, became the biggest city in Australia. At that time "a real foothold of civilization had been established," and many hunters for gold "became part of the normal community." Unfortunately, "the lot of the Chinese was unhappy." Tumbull adds:

> In 1857 there was estimated to be as many as twenty-five thousand of these peaceful people on the Victorian goldfields alone. They excited the animosity of the chauvinistic and the fear of those who looked upon them as a source of cheap-labor competitors in the fluctuations of the economy. The horror, in some cases superstitious, with which the Chinese were regarded by some of their fellow citizens in Australia, crystallized in the form of immigration restriction acts and in a considerable part of the "White Australia" thinking.

In the development of the country "the Aborigines had no part" (Tumbull, 1966). They were to "most Australians merely Stone Age men." The Aborigines

53

were almost exterminated "in the more populous Australian states" through "instances of individual cruelty, massacres and the like and the deliberate hunting of blacks by sharpshooters (the equivalent of the Europeans calipers in North America)." However these "pioneering traditions did not die and are fading away slowly." After World War II, Italians, Poles, Dutch, Germans, Greeks, Latvians, Lithuanians, Ukrainians, Yugoslavs, Hungarians, Czechs and others arrived and "altered the racial constitution of the Australian population." The migrants were originally predominantly from the United Kingdom and Ireland, and the newer immigrants created ethnic diversity in Australia.

The British Parliament passed an Act federating the separate colonies into a Commonwealth of Australia in 1900. The capital was Melbourne until 1927 when Canberra became the capital. Australia adopted the American constitutional principles of federalism yet accommodated the British parliamentary system. All matters which "most closely affected the lives of the people" including "the control of the police" (Turnbull, 1966) were concerns of the six States. In Australia the States are "largely self-contained natural regions." They have a "degree of political sovereignty," although "they may not have as much autonomy as the states of the U.S.A." (Miller and Jinks, 1971). In the U.S., roads, schools and police are "provided by locally responsible bodies," but in Australia a tradition developed of "administrative centralism" because of the growth of "wide, sparsely-settled areas" in which communities shared expenses. In this country individual States provide "the police forces and courts of justice, the homes for delinquents. . .the state mans the police station, the court house" and the state is also responsible for liquor laws and "for a variety of matters that excite public comment." Sawer (1977) mentions "the federal character obtrudes itself on the most casual visitor." Police services wear different uniforms in different areas and the Commonwealth Police Force, the Australian Federal Police (AFP), has expanded since 1901 as the "power and importance of the federal government has been increasing."

54

European colonization of New Zealand in the first half of the nineteenth century was motivated by the "commercial extension of the Australian frontier and the purposive establishment of choice English colonies" (Cameron, 1965). Unlike the Aborigines, who retreated into the bush as colonization expanded in Australia, the Maori (the original native) "fought for his land" in two wars (McLeod, 1968). Moreover, New Zealand was not "a convict settlement" with "the stultifying effects of a military oligarchy, a sullen work force, and a controlling bureaucracy located at a distant hemisphere." Arguing that "a great deal of the history of the nation is grounded in its economic history," Cameron claims that New Zealanders have been "overwhelmingly" dedicated to maintaining "prosperity and a high standard of living." The Treaty of Waitangi led Britain to declare New Zealand a crown colony, and "the first systematic colonizers in 1840" arrived, followed by "more people" after the gold rushes in California in 1848 and in Victoria and New South Wales in 1851. New Zealand is a welfare state, "the end product of centuries of struggle for social justice," but New Zealanders tend to conform to "patterns of living which are the expression of a narrow, comfortable, but nevertheless mediocre materialism." According to Rowe and Rowe (1968), "materialistic culture" in New Zealand is so strong that possessions are "no longer the symbols of good or satisfying life; they were the good life itself."

After World War II, the immigration of Polynesians, including Samoans, Cook Islanders, Tongans, and Niueans began "helping to enrich New Zealand urban life." Subsequently, these other racial or national groups have been "completely swallowed by the dominant culture of the nation." As a result, "the Bohemians of Puhoi, the Swiss or Poles of Taranaki, the Scandinavians of the Wairarapa, the French of Akaroa, and the Germans of Nelson" are not distinguishable from "the average New Zealander." New Zealand seems "more English than other former English colonies," and after becoming independent as the Dominion of New Zealand, the country continued a close association with

55

England. But, in fact, New Zealand was always more obviously willing than Australia to leave policy decisions to the United Kingdom. New Zealand was the last dominion to take advantage of the freedom of independent action conferred upon the Dominions by the Statute of Westminster of 1931. The Statute was adopted by New Zealand only in 1947 to enable the Government to carry out a purely domestic constitutional change.

Rowe and Rowe (1968) comment that "the comparative homogeneity" is due to their "predominately British origin." Although New Zealand is a bi-racial society and the Maori are proud of "a different cultural heritage from the Pakeha," (the white people), "racial prejudice does exist." Prejudice seems much better controlled in New Zealand than in other countries, because "the Maoris were apparently regarded as superior to any other aboriginal race with which the British Empire had come in contact" (Adams, 1977). An American observer (Ausubel, 1965) claims that race relations in New Zealand were "generally much better than in the United States." However, they were not as "good" as people claimed they were.

In 1875 the central government established New Zealand as a politically unified country by "abolishing the squabbling provincial councils." Without a written constitution, a situation similar to the United Kingdom, New Zealand also has laws similar to thos̲ ̲ ̲ ̲ ̲d. The national parliament is a particularly vigorous example of democratic ̲ ̲ ̲ ̲ ̲f "the relative weakness of non-parliamentary pressure groups, pre-eminence of statute law, and a remarkable degree of political awareness and activity among ordinary citizens." Moreover, the electorate is small. A privileged landed class never developed in New Zealand because of the land policies during the nineteenth century including a separate Maori system of title to land. No "administrative elite," "no old boy net, no amateur college tradition," and "no special class consciousness" exists. New Zealanders "desire to have social equality at all costs." They practice the "safety of conformity." "Slums are non-existent," and "the seeds of the Welfare State lie

56

deep in the country's history." In New Zealand people have constructed a society that is as classless "as it is possible to find anywhere" (Rowe and Rowe, 1968). Social, economic and political security has been " the over-riding preoccupation of New Zealand life" (McLeod, 1968). Adhering to "conformity," stifling "substantial cultural innovation or modification," inhibiting "extremism," and discouraging radicalism, New Zealand has developed its own "national ethos or culture." McLeod writes:

> Notwithstanding, nothing approaching the Australian concept of mateship has evolved; in its place there is a cooperative disposition. A sense of partnership substitutes for the fraternal identification that characterizes the mateship of the Australian outback, and this partnership concept is generalized into the pervasive egalitarianism of the nation.

Referring to the New Zealand schools, Gibbons (1981) describes "an uncritical course in political socialization, close to indoctrination" taught to young students in the 1920s. A textbook prescribed that the first duty of the citizen was to obey the laws, "to assist the police," and treat them with respect.

In contrast to the serene evolution of an isolated New Zealand is the volatile historical experience with the hardships of the outback in Australia. Tens of thousands of "unwilling immigrants" including "political prisoners" (Francis, 1981) were sent to the outback. The Australian settlers included convicts, Chartists, emancipists and free settlers. In Australia "political culture" was also historically diversified in the "early coastal settlements" in Sydney, Melbourne, Hobart, Adelaide, Brisbane and Swan River, now Perth. The "accompanying political structures were inevitably autonomous and self-contained" (Holmes and Sharman, 1977), and "political conflicts" occurred over "historical, territorial boundaries." Finn (1987) claims that "Victoria's colonial politics were raw, occasionally riotous, and ultimately ruinous." In the expansion of the frontiers in the Australian bush, numerous conflicts of "calumny, hatred, and strife" occurred involving racial and national "bigotry" (McLeod, 1968). "The whites successfully pursued ruthless annihilation policies at an early stage against the indigenous inhabitants of the continent" (Howard, 1980). New Zealand avoided "the problems of a multiethnic community" through a "variety of stringent immigration laws and regulations."

With the establishment of the penal colonies, Australian police were established as a paramilitary force. The mounted police corps was founded in 1820 in Australia "to repress the natives often by brutal means" (Allan, 1945) and was a "valuable and efficient body in keeping down crime in the colony generally." Men "picked from the British army, armed with saber, carbine and pistols. . .were the principals in many daring exploits against bushrangers." Victoria police were founded in 1852 as an entity independent of the New South Wales police force. The police in New Zealand were founded in 1867 as an Armed Constabulary to serve in the Second Maori War and to perform normal duties. The unarmed national police force was established in 1886 to perform police duties only.

In the state of Victoria, currently approximately 11, 502 police personnel work in a population of approximately 3.8 million. The 2000 census recorded New Zealand, population as 3.8 million, and the police number approximately 8,613. This includes 6, 808 sworn officers and 1, 805 non-sworn officers (Miller, 1996). The New Zealand police had a substantial increase in police personnel in the first part of the 1990s. This was due primarily to a policy directed to control a rising crime rate and a government interested in providing services (Miller, 1996). The police in Australia are basically the responsibility of the States, while New Zealand has a national police force. Both Australian and New Zealand police were organized like English police by the colonial administrations (Swanton, Hanigan and Psaila, 1985), and their structure sets them "apart from the British and American counterparts, which are overwhelmingly local in character" (Miller and Jinks 1971). Unlike the police in New Zealand, Australian police carry arms "which distinguishes them from English police but do not often use them (which distinguishes them from the police in the United States)." Due to historical and social reasons, "the patterns of violence" in Australia "show great similarity to those of the United States" (Braithwaite, 1990).

Politics and the police

In 1886 the New Zealand government passed the *Police Force Act*. In 1898 Superintendent J. B. Tunbridge of the London Metropolitan police became the Commissioner of New Zealand Police. He brought the police closer to the political philosophy and reforms of English police. The Australian police service is divided into six States, the Northern Territory and the Australian Federal Police, which also police the Australian Capital Territory. The New South Wales Police Service dates back to 1789 and currently is the largest police force in Australia with over 13,000 police officers. In mid-1998 Australia had approximately 43,000 police officers serving the entire country. Australian police forces are predominately male with only 16 percent of the force being female (Sarre, 1999).

In Victoria the police (1986) link the "honor and dignity" and "the responsibilities and privileges" of the office of the constable to "the historical development of peace, order and good government in England." According to Miller and Jinks (1971), "each force is controlled by a Commissioner, who has an independent status subject usually to ultimate direction by the Premier," or the political head of government in each Australian State. However, the political independence of the police seems to be honored more in New Zealand than in Australia. The Chief Commissioner, the leader of the New Zealand National Police, is selected by the national government from among the candidates nominated by the outgoing incumbent. Consequently, the police retain a considerable control over their future leaders. In Japan, the outgoing leader of the national police also participates in the selection of his successor, and his participation is attributed to political and administrative respect for police integrity and professionalism.

During the observer author's visit to Melbourne in 1987, intense discussion occurred as to who would succeed the outgoing Chief Commissioner. It was widely rumored that the State government was going to appoint somebody from outside of Australia. Senior police administrators privately suggested (Phelan, 1987) that Victoria's politicians wanted an outsider as the new Chief Commissioner, because he could be politically manipulated. In 1972 the Government of South Australia hired Harold Salisbury, a well-reputed Chief Constable from England to lead the local state police, but he was fired by the government in 1978 in what Cockburn (1979) describes as a "political assassination." Cockburn adds that, according to a British observer, Salisbury had "honesty, integrity and professional ability," but he seemed to lack the "political experience, expertise, and the political acumen to match the Australian scene." Salisbury apparently was unable to handle the situations in South Australia where "political pressures were greater and more complex" than in his native England.

Finn (1987) states that Victoria's Public Service had "little prospect of achieving those standards of efficiency and effectiveness to which the British reformers were aspiring." Many aspects of Public Service "recruitment, particularly under La Trobe, had been less than discerning," and "the reforming recommendations" of Royal Commissions and boards of enquiry, "even when acted upon, were given no great opportunity to work." In spite of the *Civil Service Act of 1862*, "political patronage in recruitment" and "political influence in promotion, deleteriously affected the quality and organization of the service." In the modern Australian bureaucracy "the emergence of an administrative elite in Canberra" has occurred, and "there is no clear distinction between policy and administration, between the political and the bureaucratic. There is no "proper distribution of power and authority."

Police unions have been historically "powerful forces" in New Zealand and Australia (Milburn, 1966). This is still true in the first decade of the twenty-first century (Dixon, 1999: 139). In New Zealand "ideological or ethnic cleavages" have not affected trade unionism, while in Australia "where greater ethnic and regional diversity has existed than in New Zealand, there has been more dissension." In Victoria, the Police Association has fought against the government. The Police Association, in a poster campaign, defeated the *Criminal Investigation Bill* of the Whitlam Federal Government in 1973. Haldane (1986) states that the "senior management people were subjected to the sting of a changing and increasingly militant police union" in Victoria. Victoria Police Association officials maintained that the police had not traditionally had a respected voice in political campaigns, and politicians were able to ignore police issues. According to them, the legislation instituting a Public Complaint Authority to investigate complaints against the police represented a continuing political apathy toward the police. It appeared to the observer author that the police union activities in this Australian State seemed very aggressive and vituperative to attain popular support and political power. Militant actions were evidently the outcome of frustrations confronted by the police in achieving their objectives.

In New Zealand the sense of frustration and bitterness was much less visible. To the observer author it appeared that a buoyancy and ebullience characterized the police union agenda in Wellington, during the general elections of 1987, when the initial study of the police was conducted. The Police Association carried on an aggressive, politically planned campaign to bargain for an increase of police personnel and to oppose the employment of part-time police officers. Palmer (1986) states that the police in New Zealand have a "well-organized and vociferous service organization" that "commands more media attention than most trade unions." The police in New Zealand were involved in a "minefield" of "law and order issues." Very often "highly simplistic views which were expressed by individuals and groups "couched in extreme language" prompted politicians to make an "immediate political response." Palmer adds:

> Politicians tend to reflect such sentiments. They defend the values implicit in the concept of law and order. They have a habit of asking for more public and community support for the police. Most

political discussions on policing, accordingly, tend to end up as a sort of auction about who support the police most. In such an atmosphere, critical comments about police behavior tend to meet powerful reaction, and accusations that particular politicians are "anti-police" are a powerful tool in the political game of discrediting one's opponents.

In New Zealand, general elections were held during the observer author's visit in 1987, to elect a new national government. Issues of law and order dominated the elections, as *The Evening Post* of July 28 indicated:

> New Zealand would soon have a further 50 police officers, Police Minister Ann Hercus announced in New Plymouth last night... she assured the meeting that the re-election of Labor would mean a continued active approach to law and order... The National Party was also promising to increase police numbers by 1000 if elected in three weeks... The association (New Zealand Police Association) was running a campaign to demand extra 1000 officers.

In the August eighth issue of the same paper, the Police Association was quoted as stating, "it intended to make law and order an election issue." Its advertisements in metropolitan papers "featured a cricket bat, helmet and German shepherd dog under the banner "Things you will need if the government does not increase police numbers." The paper added:

> The Police Association is making no apologies for the political nature of its hard-hitting advertising campaign for more officers. Its president... insisted the Association was engaging in issues politics, not party politics.... Police officers had not yet heard the firm commitment they wanted from national and Labor on the call for 1000 more officers.

Such comments as, "it is clear that both parties have felt the need to respond to public concern about violent crime," appeared in *The Dominion* of July twentieth. Both parties outdid each other with tough talk on crime. The paper added that "National's emphasis seems to be on keeping the streets, the suburbs, and the cities of New Zealand safe for New Zealanders... the recent police initiative in Hamilton, supported by Police Minister Ann Hercus is encouraging."

The new initiative referred to a new police policy that domestic violence would be treated "as an arrestable offense rather than as a routine quarrel." One observer, of the election campaign wrote in *The Dominion:*

> In effect this is a repetition of the use of law and order issue by Margaret Thatcher before the 1979 British election, - a policy which helped bring her victory... Mrs. Thatcher's tough talk on crime and punishment has been followed by a 40 percent expenditure increase in real terms on law and order since 1979 — more police, more powers, more prisons. However, the attention the police received at election time is not an isolated event.

Historically, the police of New Zealand have been regarded as an important national institution, and they have carefully exploited their position in certain public postures and declarations. Founded as an Armed Constabulary with primarily military duties, New Zealand police adopted an unarmed civil image by 1898. Section 3 (1) of the *Police Act of 1958* and the *Police Regulations of 1959* make the Commissioners of Police responsible to the Minister "for the general administration and control of the police" and for causing "all members of the police to discharge their duties to the government and the public satisfactorily and efficiently." The police occupy a unique position among government agencies in New Zealand, because they are responsible to the law only in matters of enforcement. They are responsible to the Minister solely for administration and control. The principle of police autonomy seems to be honored scrupulously, and they zealously guard their autonomy. In 1903 Commissioner J. B. Tunbridge's "resignation had been precipitated by the intervention of Cabinet in Tunbridge's disciplining of staff at Nelson, and Tunbridge resigned rather than accept this intervention. He had been an outstanding commissioner" (Young, 1985). In 1955, another commissioner, E. H. Crompton, resigned after an inquiry about certain alleged acts of misconduct, although no serious charges were made. The public reaction to the police in New Zealand is in a healthy tradition of the police maintaining their good public image. Young remarks that law and order was an "important political issue in New Zealand" and consequently, that "the police force was able to realize its needs for increased resources."

Two academics (Cameron and Young, 1987) mentioned that the police were a very stable, strong institution in New Zealand and that no politician wanted to be identified as soft on law and order. Consequently no acrimonious parliamentary debate occurred about the police budget. Between the Police Commissioner and the Minister of Police in the government of New Zealand, no permanent civil servant is assigned. The Commissioner enjoyed a special position of owing allegiance only to the law and not to a political authority. The police also have a legal section that has a great effect on law making. The police in New Zealand are considerably involved in lawmaking, as Palmer (1986) explains:

> It is certainly a desirable feature of the existing arrangements that the major law enforcers are not the primary generators of the legislation proposals they enforce. A search of the Annual Reports of the New Zealand Police since 1965 shows that only since 1978 have they listed the involvement of the Police Legal Section in making submissions before Parliamentary and inter-departmental committees considering legislation. . It is plain that Legal Section acts as a sort of conduit between the police and Parliament.... The police have played an important and sophisticated role in shaping the recommendations made to the Parliament... The select committee. . . accorded to the police equal status with the Justice Department as advisers.

The non-political and professional nature of the public bureaucracy in New Zealand was summarized by Chapman, Jackson, and Mitchell (1962):

> The Public Service in New Zealand is traditionally non-political and there are special devices to prevent political sympathies influencing promotion at all levels. No one would dispute the desirability of these for the lower grades of public servants but they sometimes result in senior appointments going to men with strong ideological convictions contrary to the policy of the government.... In recent years tension between the Public Service and Government has been endangered by overt opposition of the Public Service Association to the Government's policies.

In Australia historically, "an inbuilt resistance to any compulsion has left a legacy of hostility or at best neutrality in public attitude to the police" (Learmonth and Learmonth, 1968). If the principal characteristic of New Zealanders is conformity, "a healthy distrust of authority... distrust of politicians of all kinds" (Forbis, 1972) characterizes Australians because of "a spillover from convict ancestry." Their "hostility" to police "goes clear back to the convict days (and continues till now)." MacDougall (1963) says, "the Australian attitude to law is equivocal" and displays a "tendency" to look upon law and legal institutions "as unnecessary and unproductive super structures." Their attitude seems to explain why Australians are "surprisingly uncooperative with, and even contemptuous of, the police." MacDougall speculates that Australians share "an Irish resentment of authority." Traditionally, "the principal function of the police is to enforce laws against speeding, 'sly grog' (illegal sales of liquor), two-up, and other trivial offenses." Cunneen and Findlay (1986) noted that the police in Australia applied criminal sanctions "aggressively to behavior at best marginally disruptive." Spate (1968) adds that "the old Australia and mistrust of authority and the agents who enforce it" are combined with "the strong arm tactics and the reckless use of firearms" and the absence of a "fair deal" by the police to some groups including the Aborigines. Some "inevitable" corruption has helped to foster 'this distrust." According to Harding, (1970) the "police in Australia frequently fire" weapons, although they cannot be called "trigger-happy."

The lawlessness of the Australians continued into the late 1990s and if this lawlessness is ingrained into the Australian psyche there exist no reason to believe that the lawlessness will subside in the first decades of the twenty-first century. For example, the 1998 murder of a police officer, attacks on the elderly and firing of shots at a police station indicates that violence still continues in Australia (Dixon, 1999:138). Allegations of a breakdown of law and order led some Australians, including the print media, popular newspapers such as the *Sydney Morning Herald*, to get tougher on crime and provide support to the police regardless of any police misconduct they may perform. One form of police misconduct that the police historically have been "accused of corruption and of cooperation with criminals" (Miller and Jinks, 1971):

> The Australian tradition (only recently relaxed) of making gambling, drinking, prostitution, and the like into criminal offenses, in spite of toleration and participation in them by large sections of the community has provided many opportunities for corrupt practices. This situation may account, in part, for the unpopularity of the police with many Australians and the frequent complaint of police brutality. ... It is also sometimes suggested that the harsh relationships of Australia's convict past have persisted between police and public.

It was noted in the late 1980s that corruption has "saddened, or angered or even embarrassed" (Farmer, 1988) Australian police. A sensational case of corruption was the imprisonment of a former Queensland Police Commissioner (Sir Terence Lewis) on charges of bribery. He was a popular chief who generously responded to requests for information when he was still at the helm of police affairs. Those in political power and the police often confront one another over alleged police corruption and over attempts by the police to be treated professionally and with respect for their authority. Marked by competitiveness and bitterness, some of the police tactics, according to Sallmann (1986), have been directed toward defining the police as a "significant, powerful, political pressure group."

In 1994 the government of the State of New South Wales, Australia appointed Justice James Wood to investigate the police and to submit his finding in 1997. The investigation consisted of the following issues (Royal Commission into the New South Wales Police Service, 1997):

- The existence or otherwise, of systematic or entrenched corruption with the New South Wales Police Service (the service);
- The activities of the Professional Responsibilities Command;
- The system of promotions in the Service;
- The impartiality, or otherwise, of the service in relation to the investigation and prosecution of criminal activities including, but not limited to, pedophile activity;

❑   The efficacy of the internal informers policy of the Service.

The Royal Commission found several cases of corruption. For example, money seized during a drug raid was often divided between the police rather than being booked as evidence. Another example of police corruption was the "shakedown" by which police would stop and search street runners for drugs/money and either take the money or drugs from the runner. The Royal Commission found several reasons for corruption with the police service. These included a tradition of elitism among detectives, which include heavy drinking, long- meals, and associating inappropriately with known criminals. The Commission reported that corrupt monies were necessary to maintain the lifestyle of a detective. Another cause for allowing corruption to continue unabated was the "code of silence" where police officers closed their eyes to wrongdoing. There are organizational factors that can be considered contributing factors to police corruption. These factors include: the lack of support for ethical conduct; being exposed to high-risk areas of gaming, and vice that have established a precedent to corruption. Other organizational factors mentioned by the Royal Commission include the failure of the police service to discourage corruption or recognize its potential when police officers can often be compromised.

The police are found expressing "strong views" on the role of criminal law, courts, and corrections, and their views have led to "increasing polarization" between the police and other branches of the criminal justice system, "especially lawyers, in "unseemly slinging matches." Having "acquired considerable political muscle," the police seem not to believe that "governments must make balanced and politically difficult decisions."

Police powers

For decades it seemed that police powers in New Zealand seemed to be stronger than those in Australia (Hannigan, 1985). In New Zealand the police were allowed to conduct searches without warrants in cases involving drugs, firearms and offensive weapons like knives. Under Sections 57 and 57A of the *Police Act*, a police officer is allowed to take "any particulars of suspected persons" including his photograph, fingerprints, palm-prints, and foot-prints. He can "use reasonable force" as may be necessary to secure these particulars. Under the *Arms Act of 1983* every police officer was an arms officer, and in the processing of application for handguns, police recommendations are crucial."

Although random stops and street turnovers by the police are not legally permissible, some officers in Wellington resorted to such acts routinely. They enjoyed considerable discretionary powers in informal resolutions of minor disputes like shoplifting by juveniles. Under the *Maori Welfare Act of 1962*, Maori Committees "have power to authorize summary proceedings against Maoris in specified offenses" (Metge, 1976). In such cases the police do not need to intervene formally. To increase prevention and to resolve disputes informally, the police were establishing J-teams to work with juvenile delinquents and social workers to deal with offenses out of court "either by a warning from the police or by a period of oversight by the department of Social Welfare".

Complaints about the lack of police powers in New Zealand were rare. However, the Police Association in Victoria complained vehemently that police powers were curtailed for political reasons. It has been argued that Australia is ambiguous about constitutional directives concerning the guarantee of "personal protection against the abuse of powers" in such acts as "forced confession, false accusation, personal violence at the hands of government authorities" (Howard, 1980). No Parliament has ever tried to "enact a statement of basic rights and liberties." However, the tradition of Australian courts is very aggressive in "interpreting" existing constitutional provisions "regardless of what parliament or the government or the bureaucracy may think about it." In common law countries, like New Zealand, which has an unwritten constitution, parliament is supreme. Australia has a written constitution, and its courts are "highly familiar" with the limitation of the powers of any parliament "imposed by the written constitution itself." Howard comments that the "vulnerability of the general public" in Australia is very extensive in regard to some rights which are treated as fundamental rights elsewhere. There is no right of the people "peaceably to assemble." "Unpleasant confrontations in Melbourne" between the police and the public are due to the vagueness in laws "which could be used in such a way as to provoke and promote such confrontations rather than avoid them." As a result, the police are very dependent on the government's wishes. Howard claims that Australian politicians use their position in parliament "to denounce the idea that anyone else ought to have a right to peaceably assemble." However, the right of the public to assemble is unclear:

> In practice of course no one goes so far as to deny the right absolutely. The standard technique is to make the exercise of the right conditional upon the permission of an official, who is commonly the local chief of police. Since police forces very properly believe that their action should be guided by the general policy attitudes of their government, it follows that, whatever a chief of police may think privately, he will normally regard himself as bound to comply with a government directive as to sorts of assemblies, which he ought to permit.

During personal interviews (Rippon, 1987; Phelan, 1987; Baker, 1987), the observer author, found resentment expressed against the increasing erosion of police authority. The police complained that political officials would call officers to inquire about sensitive matters handled by the police. Laws requiring a prisoner's release from police custody within six hours, laws restricting the recording of names and addresses of offenders other than those involved in traffic violations, and laws prohibiting the fingerprinting and photographing of suspects created annoyance and impatience within the Victoria police department. The six-hour law was ridiculed by police union officials as typical legislation of the lawyers, by the lawyers and for the lawyers (Rippon, 1987). Following the consistent police demand, the law has now been changed (Brown, 1991). As Sallmann (1986) states, a number of recent law reform commissions, boards of inquiry and various committees in Australia have "reported adversely on standards of police behavior in the exercise of their powers." The police reaction has been "quick and vigorous" to accuse such groups of an "anti-police stance and have failing to take a responsible approach towards adequate protection of the community against crime."

The power of the police in New South Wales increased substantially after the Wood Royal Commission submitted its final report (1997). Three examples in which the legislative branch provided increased police powers are reviewed. First, the *Drug Misuse and Trafficking Amendment (Ongoing Dealing) Act, 1998* created a new criminal offense. When a drug dealer supplies illegal drugs on three more separate occasions s/he can be sentenced to a prison term of twenty years. Second, *The Crimes Amendment (Detention after Arrest) Act 1997* allows the police, the legal authority, to detain a suspect for investigative purposes between arrest and changes. Third, *The Crimes Legislation Amendment (Police and Public Safety) Act 1998* makes carrying a knife in a public place a crime, extends the power of the police to stop and search, and gives the police the authority to demand the name and address of witnesses and to remove people from public places under specific conditions (Dixon, 1999).

Historically, friction between politicians and the police was caused by the age-old rule that most police stations are also temporary prisons, "lock-ups" and looking after prisoners in police stations was thought to be a necessary aspect of police work. The police noticeably disliked being temporary custodians, and the distaste was expressed vehemently by many police officers. In Melbourne, the continual police custody of prisoners was cited as an example of government's resistance to police demands. In the late 1980s prisons have been built in Melbourne, and "the problem is not as severe as in 1987." Cells in some police stations have been dismantled (Brown, 1991).

All prisoners going to Victoria's most important prison, Pentridge (now closed), were first kept in the Russell Street police station and other suburban stations. When the police were informed of available prison space, prisoners were moved. However, the police complained that the prison authorities would leave prisoners in police jails and were slow to move them. The prison authorities denied their charges. Police officers felt frustrated that they were unable to convince politicians that attaching prisons to police stations and making police officers work like prison guards were eroding their morale. They complained that they did not join the police to act as prison officials and had not been trained as custodians. According to prison officers interviewed, only basic human values and management principles were required to handle temporary prisoners, but the police were unappeased. The observer author recalled a visit to Pentridge one night with a Police Inspector. While taking a tour of a police station, he observed the Inspector who was in charge of the evening shift, greeting prisoners with a warm smile. When asked why he was being so friendly with the prisoner, he explained that they were depressed, nervous, and desolate. Humane treatment, a friendly greeting, or a warm smile could make them a little less bitter, he added. Perhaps this was his answer to police complaints.

In the Richmond station in Melbourne, the police resented that the cells were "gazetted" for imprisonment for seven days, although there were no recreational facilities. Some officers commented that at least shower facilities were available there. In this old and congested station, the officers complained that prison cells had contributed to a lack of cleanliness of the premises. Accommodation in the station was so congested that the police criminal investigation staff had to locate their coffee room in the area set apart for interrogations by detectives. The station also lacked a social area and a fire escape. Melbourne's Collingwood police station looked better than Richmond's, but complaints about prison cells were the same, although they were "gazetted" for two days only. The officers had no social area except a small kitchen. They complained of the lack of security and the lack of accessibility of constables to their supervisors because of the extreme physical congestion in the station. The Fitzroy police station located in the Town Hall contained nine cells "gazetted" for fourteen days. Prison arrangements were despised by the officers here as well as at the Carlton police station where the cells were also "gazetted" for fourteen days.

The police also complained that the physical work to maintain the cells required the officers' valuable time. Police officers were required to impose punishment on their inmates sometimes for gross violations like the possession of syringes for injecting drugs. They felt like prosecutors as well as penal administrators. Guarding the cells and the prisoners also involved psychological games between prisoners and the police. One afternoon a constable on duty left the main cell door unlocked. The prisoners told the Officer-in-Charge of the shift, and he rewarded their good behavior by buying them pizzas. However, he asked them to be quiet about the open door, so that nobody from his shift would be penalized.

Since prisons were not a primary police station responsibility, not much attention was paid to maintaining supplies. There were complaints of the lack of blankets. Officers felt concerned that they often did not have surgical gloves to handle articles used by prisoners with infectious diseases. The meals for prisoners were prepared by the police; food was sold to the inmates at a profit for the benefit of station social clubs. Hardened convicted criminals and untried inmates were housed together, although the practice was considered harmful. Cameras monitored the activities of inmates in violation of the provisions of the *Human Rights Act*. The use of cameras has been discontinued (Brown, 1991). Visitors of inmates must come to the front desks of police stations to obtain permissions for visits, and they needed to be watched closely by the police for security reasons. This prison guard like surveillance practice, the police felt, was detrimental to police public relations. It appeared to the observer author that the police he talked to in Australia, despised the unpleasant prison work they had to do.

As against such experience of the officers in Australia, it is interesting to note that police officers in New Zealand were not encumbered, at the time of research, even with traffic responsibilities. The reason was that to the police officers there, their morale would plummet, because traffic work was not considered suitable police work and it was generally felt that the traffic department was unprofessional. Some members of the New Zealand public also mentioned to the observer author that traffic officers were not well respected

Working conditions

Historically, the lack of proper physical facilities has been a problem in Victoria. Haldane (1985) notes that the problem received serious attention from the Royal Commission early in this century:

> A first essential to a spirit of discipline, a smartness of bearing and dignity of demeanor, is the environment in which a man has to live and work, and the habits of order, cleanliness, and tidiness which satisfactory conditions engender ... The conditions prevailing to those buildings of the Victoria Police Force, which we inspected, were found to be the very antithesis of these.

According to Haldane (1985), "the wildcat 1923 Victoria Police Strike" was prompted, among other things, "by the official indifference which reduced the life of men in barracks to one of approximating squalor." Quoting from the Monash Royal Commission, he adds that the stables for the police horses seemed "to lack nothing essential to the health and comfort of their occupants." The Commission remarked that the houses for the police officers at St. Kilda Road Depot were "ancient and forlorn" and their "repelling cheerlessness, if not actual discomfort must make for discontent in any body of men compelled to share them." The "shabbiness and congestion" rendered the Russell Street Police Station "out of date as the principal station of a metropolis." The contemporary Labor government had invested much money for bricks and mortar for police buildings, but more has to be done. The resentment against the physical facilities became more intense when the police lost the powers that the last Liberal

73

government gave them. Unlike the police in Melbourne, New Zealand officers made no complaints about working conditions in the Wellington area. Although the Central Police Station was old, the officer had a large area, including a "social area." The offices of community constables, the one-man police stations, were well furnished. Members of the public could visit the constable who could offer them coffee. These community constables seemed to enjoy their contacts with the public in comfortable physical environments.

In 1994 the government of Australia received a *Report of the Review of Commonwealth Law Enforcement Arrangements* (CLEA). The Report was commissioned as part of the 1993-1994 budget process in order to provide an extensive examination of Australian law enforcement. This study was commissioned since law enforcement in Australia had grown extensively and in complexity (Chappell, 1996: 126). The CLEA review examined the following pertaining to Australian policing (1996:131):

- Identification of the Commonwealth's law enforcement objectives
- Examination of the arrangements put in place to meet these objectives
- Definition of the role and function of agencies to avoid duplication
- Maximizing cooperation between agencies
- Considering the Commonwealth's interests in the provision of common police services.

According to Dr. Chappell (1996: 145) the CLEA review suffers for depth and vision. Chappell claims that superficial information about the criminal environment was obtained which placed the CLEA review on shaky ground. Further, Chappell claims that long-range direction that should be taken by federal law enforcement was not answered. Another question, according to Chappell, that has not been answered concerns the lines of political accountability.

If certain occupational idiosyncrasies are included within the general working conditions, some similarities of experiences and views between the police in Australia and New Zealand are observable. The police in New Zealand had complained against courts, because they felt that offenders did not get proper punishments. They maintained that periodic punishments like community service awarded to juvenile offenders were not punishments at all. They maintained that public complaints about the police were mostly unfounded. Constables on patrol and those in Team Policing, a group which was under criticism for their highhanded attitudes, complained that their superiors were not responsive to their problems on the street. Constables on the street did not fully understand the departmental policies. In the Wellington police station, the rank-and-file did not understand that police administrators were trying to combine the resources of criminal investigation and the uniformed elements under a project called the Combined Policing Group.

Junior rookies in Wellington were generally assigned to foot patrols and were often confronted by groups of young people who were not respectful. These police officers felt isolated and did not display the kind of satisfaction found in the general attitude of police officers in New Zealand. As a result, these young officers, when they graduated to car patrols, avoided getting out of their patrol cars, in spite of the clear instructions that whenever a car was not engaged on a call, the officer should walk on foot. They probably developed distaste for walking because of their experience on foot patrol as junior rookies. In Victoria and New Zealand, police officers were not willing to walk into "notorious" public bars without a strong posse for fear of being assaulted.

Police psychiatrists who talked to the observer author claimed that no serious problems with divorce or alcoholism were discussed by New Zealand police. According to the senior police psychologist, the police there did not display marked subcultural tendencies that could breed cynicism, violence, and a distrust of outsiders. Stress was found only in such special groups of police officers like drug under-cover agents, anti-terrorist squads, electronic surveillance groups, and hostage negotiator teams. It has been noted that "at present, no formal program of stress management has been included in the recruit or senior personnel training courses in New Zealand Police" (Hewson and Singer, 1985). In regard to a propensity for stress, the Australian and New Zealand police were almost identical in that their stress-related problems seemed to develop from job experience.

Complaints and inquiries

During the 1970s and 1980s some inquiries were made into the alleged malpractices of the police in parts of Australia as well as New Zealand. As previously mentioned, inquires were made of the police New South Wales and Victoria in regard to malpractices committed by them. In their conversations with the observer author, numerous references to these inquiries that took place in the 1970s and 1980s in connection with police problems in Victoria, were made by police officers who considered them as a means used by politicians to humiliate them. However, the observer author noted that these inquiries were never mentioned by the police in Wellington and the adjoining areas in New Zealand. It was clear that inquiries and investigations against the police frustrated police officers in Australia who attributed them to a hostile political environment.

Most inquiries in Victoria were occasioned by charges of police corruption that had a long history. With the beginning of the gold rush, the population in Port Phillip (Victoria's former name) "leaped from seventy-five thousand, mainly in pastoral occupations, in 1851 to nearly two hundred thousand in 1853." Turnbull (1966) narrates that "with about eighty thousand people roaming around the goldfields," "the administrative machinery" was unable to handle numerous problems. He adds: "Most bitter resentment was felt at the arrogance of officials and of an often corrupt police, sometimes in league with the 'sly grog' sellers (bootleggers), for there was at first prohibition on the fields."

The mounted police were "unleashed on license hunts" (Forbis, 1972) to collect fees from miners. As the miners' resistance increased, the police grew "ever more arrogant and brutal." In one brief skirmish in Eureka, "twenty-two miners and six policemen were killed." Learmonth and Learmonth (1968) refer to "rampant" crime and corruption in the police forces during the gold rush. They mention a lack of public confidence in Victoria police because of "manifest incompetence of the police at the time of the Kelly gang," and a "police strike and near-anarchy in 1923." In contrast, historically, New Zealanders enjoy "the virtually complete absence of corruption and nepotism in public affairs." It has a "society that has seldom been shocked by a Profumo affair, a Mafia scandal, the assassination of a high governmental official, or sensational examples of corruption, amorality, treason, heresy, or malfeasance" (McLeod, 1968). New Zealand is "one of the least corrupt nations of the world" (Forbis, 1972) where "most politicians are solid, incorruptible citizens" (Jackson and Harre, 1969). McLauchlan (1987) claims the police in New Zealand have "an enviable reputation for honesty and restraint." Most inquiries in New Zealand involve police over zealousness and disregard toward departmental regulations.

In 1970, The Kaye Commission of Inquiry was appointed to inquire if members of Victoria police were extracting money from persons performing abortions. Subsequently, three officers were charged and found guilty of accepting bribes to protect the illegal activities of the abortionists. Haldane (1986) commented:

> When passing sentence Mr. Justice Starke commented, 'by your conduct you have severely shaken the community's confidence on the Victoria Police Force and inevitably I think the morale of the force itself must have been lowered.' He was right. The worst tragedy in this part of the trilogy was not that three policemen went to goal, but that their activities shrouded an entire police force in a cloud of suspicion and innuendo.

Haldane adds that the number of officers in the scandal was too large, but it raised serious ethical issues because of the length of time over which the illegal activities had flourished, the seniority of the policemen involved, and their positions in police and public life. Haldane continues: "many Victorians, including the Australian Labor Party, the Country Party, and the Democratic

Labor Party, wanted a Royal Commission" to inquire into other allegations against the police. However, the Liberal government had been a witness to "enough dirty linen washed through the press" in the abortion inquiry and did not want public exposition of more scandals. Instead Colonel Sir Eric St. Johnston, the Chief Inspector of Constabulary for England and Wales, was asked to study the practices of Victoria police. Sir Eric (1971) wrote:

> I am given to understand that, there have been allegations from time to time that personnel in Victoria Police have been corrupt and have received bribes for overlooking offenses against the law, and I am aware, of course, that this report is being written in the shadow of a public enquiry in which allegations of corruption have been leveled against certain senior serving and retired officers of the Force.

Haldane (1985) says that the report was an inquiry into "all aspects of policing in Victoria" and that it contained "in excess of 180 recommendations."

In 1975 B. W. Beach, Queen's Counsel (Q.C), was appointed to conduct an investigation of some members of Victoria police charged with criminal offenses, breaches of Standing Orders, and harassment and intimidation of members of the public. He found that fifty-five members of the police were involved in conspiracy, perjury, assault, unlawful arrest, corrupt practice of receiving money, and fabricating evidence. These were among "one hundred and thirty one complaints" (Haldane, 1985). Because Victoria police officers intensely resented the findings of Beach, the government appointed the Norris Committee, which suppressed the recommendations of the Beach inquiry. Thirty-two of the fifty-five officers cited by Beach were finally charged, but none was convicted.

In 1985 the Neesham Committee of Inquiry (1985) was requested "to conduct an urgent review of the procedures adopted in maintaining internal discipline within the Force," and it found that the Victoria Police Department lacked "a coherent disciplinary system." An Assistant Commissioner was allegedly involved in improprieties with Continental Airlines but 'the charges against the Assistant Commissioner were dropped" later (Brown, 1991).

Allegations about the suspected participation of a detective sergeant in a scandalous narcotics ring were also made in Melbourne. To the public (Braithwaite, Grabosky and Rickwood, 1986) "corruption in public life ... has been a matter of police and political payoffs" in Australia.

According to Swanton, Hannigan, and Psaila (1985), during the 1970s and 1980s several inquiries were made into complaints against New Zealand police. The Kennedy Commission of Inquiry was appointed "to inquire into certain matters relating to the conduct of the members of the police force in 1954-55." The Lason Commission of Inquiry was also instituted in 1955 "to inquire into the prosecution by the police of Donald James Raka and Murdoch Campbell Harris." In 1974 the Polynesian community established an unofficial tribunal of two Maoris, two other Polynesians and two *Pakehas* (whites) to inquire into a "police innovation, a mobile Task Force set up to deal with increasing violence in the streets and hotels of the inner city in Auckland" (Metge, 1976). It was alleged that the police were concentrating on the streets, bars and hotels frequented by racial minorities. Arrests of Maori and other Polynesians were made in disproportionate numbers by the Task Force. The Maori and the Commissioner of Police in Auckland met, and the latter 'expressed surprise and hurt at the vehement and hostility of most of the Maori speakers." According to Metge, the Commissioner would have been wise to recognize that "paternalistic enthrocentrism" of the *Pakehas* in power is itself the "major cause of disharmony." Ausubel (1965) claims that he found an "atmosphere of paternalism" in the government itself.

The Royal Commission inquired into the circumstances of the convictions of one Arthur Allan Thomas for the murders of David Harvey Crewe and Jeanette Lenore Crewe and submitted its report in 1980. The visit of the South African rugby team in 1981 caused large ugly confrontations between the police and the public in New Zealand. Allegations of police misuse of power were made, and there was a report of the Chief Ombudsman "on the investigation of complaints against the police arising from the South African Rugby tour of New Zealand in 1981." According to the Chief Ombudsman (1987), the charges were made against a "force policy rather than individual misconduct." McLauchlan (1987) notes that a "breach between the community and the service became apparent during the civil disobedience at the time of the Springbok rugby tour in 1981."

In 1951, the government had used "very tough strike-breaking tactics and emergency powers" during a wharf strike (Jackson, 1972). Following the passage of the Police Offenses Amendment Bill of 1951, which contained "harsh", measures; the New Zealand Council for Civil Liberties was formed. In 1983 another Royal Commission "to inquire into certain matters relating to drug trafficking (Stewart) was necessary. In the same year the government formed the Temm Commission for inquiry into the circumstances of the release of Ian David Donaldson from a psychiatric hospital and of his subsequent arrest and release on bail. Following the 1983 fatal shooting of Paul Chase, who was wanted in connection with an investigation regarding the discharge of a firearm in a hotel bar, C.M. Nicholson Q.C., was appointed to monitor police homicide investigations. In 1984 there was a Committee of Inquiry concerning a riot in Auckland.

While Victoria police officers complained about these investigations and inquiries, the New Zealand police never mentioned them. According to the Report of the New Zealand Police for the year ending in March 1987, which was reviewed by the observer author during the study of the police in New Zealand and Australia, there were 401 serious complaints against the police. According to the Victoria Police Annual Report ending in June 1986, there were 486 serious complaints. The number of complaints in the New Zealand jurisdiction with its smaller population and smaller force is almost as high as those in Victoria. The Chief Ombudsman (1987) in Wellington remarked that complaints were not made by minorities who normally do not complain against the police in New Zealand, because they were not aware of their rights. Interestingly, in Australia more complaints were heard from the police than the public, but in New Zealand, the public complained against the police more than in Australia, and the police never complained about the public. Moreover, the police in Australia were seemingly affected more by allegations and inquiries than New Zealand officers. The impact of allegations and complaints against the police in Victoria seemed to be greater, because Australia was more volatile and politically involved with the police.

In New Zealand the press has been "conservative in attitudes as well as standards ... pronational" (Chapman, Jackson and Mitchell, 1962). Metge (1976) notes that the press tends "to discipline itself." Ausubel (1965) referred to "the incredible conformity" of the editorial policy of newspapers" and how "controversial subjects and the dissemination of liberal views" were suppressed by the New Zealand Broadcasting Service, which was "controlled" by the government. Victoria's press, however, has been "robust, partisan, occasionally cavalier with the truth" (Finn, 1987) since the colonial days and generated "defamation actions and contempt proceedings" by politicians, judges, and "public servants, high and lowly," seeking their "vindication against allegations of venality, partiality or incompetence." In the press "Public Service and public servants inevitably were the objects of a recurrent, usually unfavorable, scrutiny." It "strongly ramifies itself into commercial radio and television, is essentially State rather than national in outlook" (Crisp, 1978). It "tends to foster a particularistic, provincial climate of opinion."

In the mid-1970s because of the way the Australian police dealt with citizen's complaints about allegations of police misconduct, the Australian Law Reform Commission (ALRC) recommended that a civilian review board, or the term currently in vogue, 'civilian oversight' review citizen complaints, against the police (Lewis and Prenzler, 1999: 1). Currently, a variety of agencies are reviewing citizen complaints against the police. Two states, New South Wales and Western Australia split the review of citizen complaints between the State Omnibus and the Police Integrity Commission (PIC). The state of Western

Australia has a Deputy Ombudsman who investigates citizen complaints against the police. Generally, the Ombudsman in the other Australian States have jurisdiction over citizen complaints. All civilian oversight review mechanisms, whether an Ombudsman, Police Integrity Commission, or some other review mechanism, either report to their respective state Parliament or to a Parliamentary Committee (Lewis and Prenzler, 1999).

In the early 1990s the New Zealand police did a study, which had as its major objective "to determine the satisfaction of crime victims and complainants with the way in which police dealt with them personally, and with their offense situation" (Boni, 1995). The study found that 81 percent of the respondents were either "satisfied" or "very satisfied" with the way in which police dealt with them personally. Females over the age of fifty and those widowed gave higher levels of satisfactions than other groups surveyed. Only seven percent of those surveyed were dissatisfied with how the police treated them. The reason most often given for satisfaction with the police was quick response by the police (24 percent) followed by police officers being friendly, courteous, or helpful (16 percent). A slow response for service was given as the primary reason for dissatisfaction (24 percent) followed by being unsympathetic (16 percent) and considering their matter as trivial or unimportant (14 percent). During the same time frame surveys of the Australian police revealed that 70 percent of citizens nationwide who had contact with the police rated them as doing a very good or good job. In the Australian Capital Territory only four percent of respondents indicated they were dissatisfied with the police because they were rude, failed to take action or lacked interests in the citizens problem. Eighty-six percent of those surveyed reported they were either very satisfied or satisfied with the police (Boni, 1995).

Morale and respectability

The difference between Victoria police, and probably the other police in Australia, and the police in New Zealand in regard to their degrees of satisfaction may be due to many other factors like recruitment, training, leadership, sociological conditions, and organizational tradition. These are considered important variables of police morale and satisfaction (Punch, 1985; Sherman, 1974, 1978; Heffernan and Stroup, 1985). However, with the police in Victoria and New Zealand, every relevant discussion of these issues centered around politics and the police. A political climate marked by seemingly aggressive resistance to police demands by those in power characterized the environment of the police in Victoria. The police aggressiveness seems to result from the fact that the police in Australia feel they must fight against heavy odds to achieve respectability, status, and authority. The politicians' resistance to the police probably reflects the public's cynicism regarding police history. Do the police have a vested interest in keeping the struggle alive? The conflicts seem to have benefited the police: the six-hour-rule the police resented no longer exists. Cells in many police stations are no longer used for incarceration. The Police Complaints Authority created in 1986 was discontinued a few years later and since 1988 a Deputy Ombudsman has been given the responsibility to review citizen complaints against the police (Lewis and Prenzler, 1999). Nevertheless, these changes have not swept away the debris of history, the tradition of corruption and public skepticism, and the stigma of the dubious practices of the past. Politically, the police seem to have succeeded in improving their status but not their moral authority, which demands greater acceptance of the police by the public.

In New Zealand the police are very highly respected public servants (Glynn, 1975) and are clearly "an important political influence" (Palmer, 1986). They enjoy "respect", and are regarded as "custodians" of law and order. Politicians in New Zealand "defend the values implicit in the concept of law and order." The police have succeeded in identifying themselves with "a whole trade of sturdy, middle-class values." More importantly, in the climate of public opinion anyone who does not support the police is likely to be called "a stirrer, a protestor, a person who represents unacceptable and unrespectable segments of New Zealand society." The politicians' support of the police is a "convenient" means of demonstrating "adherence to existing social order and a commitment to the maintenance of stability." In fact, Palmer continues, "Although the police do not actively seek this political role they know how to take advantage of the strategic position they occupy ... in order to further the aims and objectives of the police service".

The police in New Zealand, luckily, do not have to fight in a bitter struggle for recognition and status. They enjoy a kind of verve and confidence, because they can get the rights and privileges they want. In New Zealand the public seem highly satisfied with the quality of police service (Jonas and Whitfield, 1986). The awareness of the police regarding this attitude on the part of the public has made them cautious and zealous in maintaining a public image of integrity, conservatism and popular good will (Bayley, 1976). Although some subordinate officials of the police were somewhat concerned as noted by the observer author, the New Zealand police as a body supported the new legislation for a Public Complaint Authority introduced in 1987. Their support was almost an unconscious recognition of the public trust by the police in New Zealand (although, as mentioned above, the public complained about the police there more than in Australia). In Victoria the police resented the Police Complaint Authority, which was subsequently disbanded. The rank-and-file members of the police in Victoria probably intuitively sensed that the Authority would not be highly regarded by the public because of historical public skepticism against the police. It was also evident that the morale of the police in Victoria and other states was not high. In police boats and patrol cars, at police stations, training establishments, and police headquarters in Melbourne, the observer author talked with many police officers who were willing to take on premature retirement. Their frustrations and resentment were not just "political" but real.

84

Conclusions

The foregoing account was intended to discuss what appeared to an observer, the observer author in this case, as the difference in police entanglement in politics and the sense of police morale and respectability which is related to politics. It should be clear that the issues of politics, morale and respectability which have been affecting the police in Australia and New Zealand are inseparable. On one hand respectability or the lack of it, for example, affects police morale. On the other hand, politics can affect the police more if they lack respectability. If the public image of the police is bad, it is more than likely that politicians will reflect that public sentiment in their dealings with the police. Such an attitude makes the police distrustful of outsiders, public and politicians both and they become hostile to them. All this is connected with morale. Their unique history, special environment and individual challenges have shaped the police in Australia and New Zealand differently. Nevertheless, both the police have been marked by efforts to achieve greater professionalism, higher levels of service capability and stronger capacity to meet the challenges of the present time. However, the police in Australia seem to be in need of greater efforts. ·

The "limits of police reform" (Bayley, 1977) in Victoria as well as elsewhere in Australia are circumscribed primarily by historical antecedents of the police force and the social attitude toward the police as a result of the country's evolution. The Police Service Board (1979) observed:

> In a young state, such as Victoria is, the folklore of the colonial and gold rush eras lingers on as far as police functions and activities are concerned. In this respect the background differs somewhat from the United Kingdom in that the Victorian tradition is founded upon a more picturesque scene dominated by pioneering settlements ranging over very large areas with rapidly changing concentrations as gold was found and supportive rural and commercial developments occurred, latter in due course, taking over in their own right.

The image of the mounted "trooper" policing "a comparatively rugged and poorly disciplined society" still seems to haunt Australian police (Haydon, 1911).

Neither the public nor the police have forgotten this "not unimportant fact." The outdated mounted trooper as a "forerunner" of the modern police officer remains still "sufficiently recent in historical terms." According to Moore (1991), confusion also seems to characterize the Australian police mandate, which the police determine themselves to "a large degree." That "confusion about lines of accountability in Australia's 'Washminister' system of government" was often apparent in Australia where the police felt they were fighting against the meddling of politicians in police affairs. Like "many aspects of development of policing (Finnane, 1989), the problems of dissatisfaction which are connected with questions of police autonomy, of the politicalization of the police, and the nature of police powers and their legal regulations" in Victoria and in Australia require "historical investigation." In Australia "policing is a controversial public issue" (Bowden, 1978). In the early decades of the twenty-first century policing not only in the state of Victoria but also in the other states still continues to be a controversial issue.

References

Adams, Peter. 1997. *Fatal Necessity.* Auckland: Auckland University Press.

Allan, J. Alex. 1945. *Men and Manners in Australia.* Melbourne: F.M. Cheshire Pty Ltd.

Annual Report, 1986. Victoria Police. Melbourne, Victoria.

Annual Report, 1987. New Zealand Police. Wellington, New Zealand.

The Arms Act, 1983. Wellington, New Zealand.

Ausubel, David P. *1965. The Fern and the Tikki.* Chicago: Holt, Rinehart and Winston.

Baker, R.G. 1987. Personal Interview. Melbourne.

Bayley, David H. 1976. *Forces of Order: Police Behavior in Japan and the United States,* Berkeley. California: University of California Press.

1977. Limits of Police Reform. In David H. Bayley, ed. *Police and Society.* Beverly Hills, California: Sage Publications.

Boni, Nadia. 1995. *Perceptions of Police and Policing: A Review of Public and Private Surveys.* Payneham, SA: National Police Research Unit.

Bowden, Tom. 1978. *Beyond the Limits of the Law.* Ringwood, Victoria Penguin Books Ltd.

Braithwaite, John. 1990. Personal Interview. Baltimore, MD.

Braithwaite, John, Pete Grabosky, and Debra Rickwood. 1986. Research Note: Corruption Allegations and Australian Business. Regulation. *Australian and New Zealand Journal of Criminology* 19: 179-186.

Brown, Gavin. 1991. Personal Correspondence. Melbourne.

Cameron, Neil and Warren Young. 1987. *Policing at Crossroads.* Wellington: Allen & Unwin.

1987. Personal Interview. Wellington.

Cameron, William J. 1965. *New Zealand.* Englewood Cliffs, New Jersey: Prentice Hall, Inc.

Chapman, P.M., W.K. Jackson, A.V. Mitchell. 1962. *New Zealand Politics in Action.* Wellington: Oxford University Press.

Chappell, Duncan (1996) "A Review of Federal Law Enforcement Arrangements," in Duncan.

Chappell and Paul Wilson, *Australian Policing: Contemporary Issues,* Second edition. Sydney, Australia: Butterworth.

Cockburn, Stewart. 1979. *The Salisbury Affair.* Melbourne: Sunbooks PTY. Ltd.

Committee of Inquiry, Victoria Police Force. 1987. *Report of the Committee of Inquiry.*

Melbourne: Ministry for Police and Emergency Services.

Crisp, L.F. 1978. *Australian National Government.* Melbourne: Longman Cheshire P.U.C. Ltd.

Cunneen, Chris and Mark Findlay. 1986. The Functions of Criminal Law in Riot Control. *Australian & New Zealand Journal of Criminology* 19: 163-178.

The Dominion. 1987. Wellington, New Zealand.

The Evening Post. 1987. Wellington, New Zealand.

Dixon, David. 1999. *A Culture of Corruption: Changing an Australian Police Service.* Annandale, NSW: Hawkins Press.

Farmer, Roy. 1988. Corruption as a Regional Problem. *Police Studies* 11(1), 14-17.

Finn, Paul. 1987. *Law and Government in Colonial Australia.* Melbourne: Oxford University Press.

Finnane, Mark. 1989. Police Rules and Organization of Policing in Queensland. *Australian & New Zealand Journal of Criminology* 22: 95-108.

Forbis, William H. 1972. *Inside Australia.* New York: Harper & Row.

Francis, Ronald D. 1981. *Migrant Crime in Australia.* St. Lucia: University of Queensland Press.

Gibbons, P.J. 1981. The Climate of Opinion. In W.H. Oliver and B.P. Williams, eds. *The Oxford History of New Zealand.* Wellington: Oxford University Press.

Glynn, J.F. 1975. *The New Zealand Policeman.* Wellington: Institute of Public Administration.

Haldane, Robert. Victoria. 1985. In Bruce Swanton, Carry Hannigan, and Trish Psaila, eds. *Police Source Book* 2. Phillip ACT: Australian Institute of Criminology.

1985. Wildcat-1923 Victoria Police Strike. In Bruce Swanton, Carry Hannigan, and Trish Psaila, eds. *Police Source Book* 2. Phillip ACT: Australian Institute of Criminology.

1986. *The People Force: A History of the Victoria Police.* Canton, Victoria: Melbourne University Press.

Hannigan, Carry. 1985. "Legal Powers and Prosecution." In Bruce Swanton, Carry Hannigan, and Trish Psaila, eds. *Police Source Book 2.* Phillip ACT: Australian Institute of Criminology.

Harding, R. W. 1970. *Police Killings in Australia.* Ringwood, Victoria: Penguin Books Ltd.

Haydon, A.L. 1911. *The Trooper Police of Australia.* London: Andrew Melrose.

Heffeman, William C. and Timothy Stroup, eds. 1985. *Police Ethics: Hard Choices in Law Enforcement.* New York: The John Jay Press.

Hewson, Victor A. and Ming S. Singer. 1985. "Type A Behavior in New Zealand Police." *Police Studies 8* (2), 97-100.

Holmes, Jean and Campbell Sherman. 1977. *Australian Federal System.* Hormby, Australia: George Allen & Unwin Australia P.U.C. Ltd.

Howard, Cohn. 1980. *The Constitution, Power and Politics.* Melbourne: The Dominion Press.

Jackson, Keith and John Harre. 1969. *New Zealand.* New York: Walker and Company.

Jackson, W.K. 1972. *New Zealand Legislative Council.* Toronto: University of Toronto Press.

Jonas, Arthur B.J. and Elizabeth Whitfield. 1986. Postal Survey of Public Satisfaction with Police Officers in New Zealand. *Police Studies* 9(4), 211-221.

Learmonth, Andrew and Nancy Learmonth. 1968. *Encyclopedia of Australia.* London: Frederick Warne & Co., Ltd.

Lewis, Colleen and Tim Prenzler (1999) "Civilian Oversight of Police in Australia," Trends and Issues in Crime and Criminal Justice, *Australian Institute of Criminology.*

MacDougall, D.J. 1963. "Law." In A.L. McLeod, ed. *The Pattern of Australian Culture.* New York: Cornell University Press.

McLeod, A.L. 1968. Introduction. In A.L. MacLeod, ed. *The Pattern of New Zealand Culture.* New York: Cornell University Press.

McLauchlan, Gordon. 1987. *Encyclopedia.* Auckland, New Zealand: David Bateman Ltd.

Metge, Joan. 1976. *The Maoris of New Zealand.* London: Routledge & Kegan Paul.

Milburn, Josephine F. 1966. "Trade Unions in Politics in Australia and New Zealand," *The Western Political Quarterly* XIX (4), 672-687.

Miller, Iran. 1996. *Demography and Attrition in the New Zealand Police 1985-95.* Wellington, New Zealand: New Zealand National Police Headquarters.

Miller, J.D.B. and Brian Jinks. 1971. *Australian Government and Politics.* London: Gerald Duckworth & Co. Ltd.

Moore, David B. 1991. Origins of Police Mandate: The Australian Case Reconsidered. A paper presented at the Academy of Criminal Justice Annual Meeting in Nashville, Tennessee, -23.

The Neesham Committee of Inquiry. 1985. Report of the Committee of Inquiry: Victoria Police Force. Melbourne. Government Printer.

Palmer, Geoffrey. 1986. "The Legislative Process and the Police." In Neil
Cameron and Warren Young, eds. *Policing at Crossroads.* Wellington:
Allen & Unwin.

Phelan, Barry. 1987. Personal Interview. Melbourne, Australia.

The Police Act. 1987. Wellington, New Zealand.

The Police Regulations. 1959. Wellington, New Zealand.

Police Service Board. 1979. *Report.* Victoria: Melbourne, Australia

Punch, Maurice. 1985. *Conduct Unbecoming: Social Construction of Police
Deviance and Control.* London: Tavistock Publications.

Rippon, Thomas. 1987. Personal Interview. Melbourne, Australia.

Rowe, Jones W. and Margaret A. Rowe. 1968. *New Zealand.* New York: Fredrick
A. Praeger, Inc.

Royal Commission into the New South Wales Police Service (1997) Final Report
Volume 1: Corruption, The Government of the State of New South Wales.

Sarre, Rick (1999) "Policing" in Sarre, Rick and Tomaino, J. Editors *Exploring
Criminal Justice: Contemporary Australian Themes.* Adelaide, Institute of
Justice Studies.

Sallmann, Peter A. 1986. Perspectives on the Police and Criminal Justice Debate.
In Chappel, Duncan and Paul Wilson, eds. *The Australian Criminal
Justice System: The Mid-1980.* Sydney: Butterworths.

Sawer, Geoffrey. 1977. *Australian Government Today.* Melbourne: Melbourne
University Press.

Sherman, Lawrence W. 1978. *Scandal and Reform: Controlling Police
Corruption.* Berkeley, CA: University of California Press.

1974. *Police corruption A Sociological Perspective.* New York: Doubleday.
Spate, O.H.K. 1968. *Australia.* New York: Frederick A. Praeger, Inc.

St. Johnston, Sir. Eric. 1971. *A Report on the Victoria Police Force.* Melbourne:
Government Printer.

Swanton, Bruce, Carry Hannigan, and Trish Psaila, eds. 1985. *Police Source Book* 2. Phillip, ACT: Australian Institute of Criminology.

The Chief Ombudsman. 1987. Personal Interview, Wellington, New Zealand.

Young, Sherwood. 1985. "New Zealand." In Bruce Swanton, Turnbull, Clive. 1966. *The Concise History of Australia.* London: Thames and Hudson Ltd.

Carry Hananigan, and Trish Psaila eds. *Police Source Book* 2. Phillip ACT; Australian Institute of Criminology.

*The authors gratefully acknowledge the contribution of Dr. Rick Sarree, Dr. Tim Prenzler and Dr. Greg Newbold in revising and updating the chapter.

Chapter 3

Policy and Practice of Multiculturalism
The Canadian Police

Introduction

The observer author received a grant from the Canadian Studies Program to study multiculturalism and the Canadian police. Unlike in the previous chapter in which the theme of "politics, morale and respectability" emerged accidentally through observations of the police in Australia, the focus and the objective of the present chapter were decided before the beginning of the actual field research in Montreal, Oakville, Ottawa, and Toronto. This study was undertaken to understand police policy and practice in regard to the ethnic groups for which we have used the Canadian term, "visible minority".

The chapter opens with a discussion of the multicultural and multiracial position of the Government of Canada conveyed by some national statutes, government's policies and official pronouncements. The policies and actions of the provincial governments as well as the municipal approaches to the issues of multiculturalism are briefly analyzed. This is followed by a discussion on the police stand on and their officially proclaimed strategy toward the ethnic minority population in the country. In order to compare what officially exist as the laws and the policies governing actions of the government and those of the police in regard to their treatment of the ethnic population, a review of the literature has been presented in this paper. This has been undertaken for elucidating the instances of discrimination, abuse of authority and other forms of injustice in books and articles written on the subject. After a discussion of the various challenges that the police under review are confronted with, recommendations have been presented how the police can narrow the gap between the policy and practice in the area of multiculturalism, with concluding thoughts that progress in protection of the rights and dignity of the minority communities can be made through combined action primarily between politicians, administrators, and the police.

The fieldwork took place in the 1992-93 and it is more than a decade since the actual study was completed. However, in the process of the revision for the new book, a more updated literature review has been accomplished with a view to exploring the extent of changes in the Canadian situation in the area of multiculturalism. The manuscript was also read by a number of Canadian scholars and practitioners who were asked to critically review the observations, comments and the analyses. The challenges of multiculturalism remain live and intractable in today's Canada too.

Research methodology

Questionnaires were distributed to police officers in Montreal, Toronto and Ottawa asking their views on various aspects of the minority issue: What the police thought were problems of the minority in their relationship with the society and, with the police. The responses received through the questionnaires were tabulated and the information gathered is stated as views of police officers based on the questionnaires.

The observer author accompanied police officers on patrol in the various ethnic pockets in these cities besides another location, namely, Halton Regional Police Service near Toronto which gave him an opportunity to discuss the same questions. Instead of distributing the questionnaire, the observer author discussed the questions with the officers accompanying him. He also visited police offices where he was able to interview police executives and asked the same questions. In most case their names have not been mentioned because of their request for anonymity.

94

The Police Chiefs and the other staff in Montreal, Ottawa and Toronto police departments were very cooperative. The Chief Inspector in charge of the observer author's visit to the police department in Ottawa was so keen on his learning about the police and minorities from as many sources as possible that he paid the registration fees for a seminar on race relations which was organized by a non-police group in the city during the time of the visit. Numerous patrol companions explained to the observer author their views on the police and policing. No questionnaires were administered to the police officers in the Halton Regional Police Service. The observer author was mainly in contact with Chief of Police James Harding in that police department. He arranged for the observer author to discuss various questions regarding the minority and the police with Clare Lewis, Chairperson of the Race Relations and Policing Task Force of Ontario. During the summer of 1991, the researcher spent a few days with the police in Vancouver, British Columbia, researching the problems of police and ethnic relations.

Review of multicultural policy
A review of government policy, official position

Instead of adopting an ideology of the American melting pot, Canada has adopted multiculturalism as an avowed public policy in its *Charter of Rights and Freedoms. The Canadian Multiculturalism Act of 1988* declares that "the policy of the Government of Canada" is to "recognize and promote ... multiculturalism" as reflecting "the cultural and racial diversity of Canadian society" and as "a fundamental characteristic of Canadian heritage and identity." Canadian multiculturalism signifies that Canada (Lederman, 1981) has a "distinct society in North America which differs in vital ways from that of the United States." To preserve this distinctiveness "all Canadians including those of British and French origin, should hold together in a federal Canada, separate from the United States." Although Canada has been moving "intellectually and culturally" toward the United States increasing "the distance between us (Canada) and our British and European heritage," it will never "become a complete carbon copy of the United States." Goldberg (1986) states:

> In urban areas the myth manifests itself in the very distinctive way we view agglomerations of different ethnic groups. In Canada we call them ethnic neighborhoods. The neighborhood metaphor works: the American metaphor of ghetto does not work. American ghettos are viewed as aberrations, since they have not melted, whereas in Canada these strongly ethnic neighborhoods are viewed as essential elements in the urban cultural mosaic.

Weinfeld (1985) mentions that "ethnic survivalism has enjoyed greater historical dominance in Canada than in the States." Unlike the American Constitution's assurance of "a universal vision of free and equal citizens," the *Canadian British North American Act of 1867* "legitimizes group particularism." It recognizes the unique language and cultural rights of the two Canadian "charter" groups — the English and the French. This recognition facilitates "the principles of a legally accepted and socially desirable affirmation of ethnic origin" to all immigrant groups in Canada. It has led to the acceptance of "a vision of Canada, as a bilingual, bicultural nation of two founding peoples to a multicultural country with equality for all cultural and racial communities within a bilingual framework" (Miner, 1986). At the turn of the century, the Canadian Prime Minister Wilfrid Laurier promised to "build a nation great among the nations of the world" from diverse elements. Later, Pierre Trudeau reiterated that "Canadian identity will not be undermined by multiculturalism" and that "cultural pluralism" was "the very essence" of Canada's identity.

As Fleras et al (1989) summarized, the protection of minority culture and identity is an important facet of the Canadian philosophy of governance. They say that "ethnocultural differences" are no longer "dismissed as inimical to national identity and unity," and their "presence is promoted as an inevitable and desirable component of the social fabric." In response to the *Report of the Royal Commission on Bilingualism and Biculturalism*, the Citizenship Branch of the Department of the Secretary of State has commissioned "histories specifically directed to the background, contributions and problems of various cultural groups in Canada" (Abu-Laban, 1980). Now Canadians have begun to "recognize ethnic diversity as a rich resource" instead of "a problem." "The increased interest of Canadian scholars in ethnic relations" is partly due to "the development of state policy over the past two decades" (Frideres, 1989).

Historically, "the real essence of the Canadian federal union is thus cultural duality of Canada ... the compact between two cultures, two nations, English and French" (Brown, 1969). In recent years, Guindon (1988) states, "the French Canadian culture has been more aggressive and forceful" within the traditional "cultural dualism" because of "the social and cultural factors." Traditionally, Canadian politicians have (Stewart, 1986) "tried to ameliorate Canada's ethnic and religious tensions." "The nationalism of the French Canadians," their concern for their "language rights," and their "solidarity" have been "complicating" Canadian politics. However, "Canadian society was much more democratic, less disciplined by class and deference, and more geographically dispersed than British society." Multiculturalism is a product of "the emerging Anglo-Canadian nationalism." It "fills the void" in the absence of "any consensus on the substance of Canadian identity or culture ... national characteristics."

According to King (1997), the aboriginal protest movement has had positive impacts on their right to govern themselves. By their protests aboriginals were able to transfer these activities to constructive programs by "pursuing their goals of self-determination and self sufficiency". Aboriginal communities have also taken control of their own schools, child-welfare programs and agencies, economic development and crisis interventions programs, and justice system (Long, 1995).

In 1975 Quebec "moved into the main stream of human rights legislation

97

in the western world by enacting as a statute the *Charter of Human Rights and Freedoms* (Lederman, 1981). According to the *Policy Statement on Race Relations,* the Government of Ontario "has for many years valued and fostered the development in Ontario of a multicultural and multiracial society." It adds that "racial and ethnic diversity has enriched the lives of all Ontario residents." Written by the Standing Committee on Multiculturalism in June 1987, *Multiculturalism: Building the Canadian Mosaic* (Quoted by Jam, 1988) states that "six provinces have multicultural policies." Saskatchewan has had a *Multiculturalism Act* since 1974, and four other provinces have "legislation that relates to multiculturalism." Five provinces have "cabinet committees" on multiculturalism, and one has "a senior interdepartmental committee." Jam notes that Manitoba and Nova Scotia have included visible minorities "in employment equity programs for civil service." To effect multicultural objectives within municipal governments, the Federation of Canadian Municipalities adopted in 1986 "a policy" for improving race relations in Canadian municipalities and sponsored a national symposium on race relations in the same year. In 1987 the Federation established a national committee on race relations. Nationally the *Canadian Charter of Rights and Freedoms* applies to all jurisdictions.

Police position and policies

It is logical that the country's official commitment toward multiculturalism will undoubtedly be reflected by Canada's police strategies and approaches. Following a national symposium on policing in multicultural communities organized by the Multicultural Directorate in 1984, the Canadian Association of the Chiefs of Police has been supporting, with funds from the government, a National Police Multiculturalism Liaison Standing Committee. The Committee is composed of visible minority community representatives and selected police chiefs to improve police work with minorities (Jam, 1988). The Canadian Multiculturalism Committee, established by the federal government to advise the Secretary of State, has a police chief as a member. A national advisory committee has been formed to assist the Commissioner of the Royal Canadian Mounted Police to implement a policy for ensuring "visible minorities" in policing (RCMP Commissioner Inkster quoted by Samuel, 1988).

According to a former Chief of Police in Montreal (Bourget, 1987), minority relations for the Montreal police (*Communaute Urbaine de Montreal*) are a central concern embracing the fundamental values, moral standards, and police respect for the rights of citizens established in the *Canadian Charter of Rights and Freedoms*. In pursuance of its Race Relations Policy, the Metropolitan Toronto Police Services Board has stated in its Standing Order No. 24 that "every member of the Force must avoid any expression or display of prejudice, bigotry; discrimination, and sexual or racial harassment." Before the Race Relations and Policing Task Force in 1989, the Government of Ontario has commissioned six reports on issues concerning the police and minorities. In Ontario the Police Development and Coordination Branch of the Ministry of the Solicitor General has been arranging cross-cultural and race relations training for the police. The *Ontario Police Services Act of 1991* incorporates many of the recommendations of the Race Relations and Policing Task Force headed by Clare Lewis who commented (1989) that Canadian police are well liked by the people.

The Halton Regional Police Service displays the "Minister's Award for Excellence in Race relations" that it received in 1991 from the Ministry of Multiculturalism and Citizenship for "the exemplary contribution toward elimination of racism and racial discrimination in Canada." The Halton Regional Police Service (Harding, Personal Conversation, 1991) indicated that willingness by public institutions had been expressed to assist the police in enhancing understanding with visible minorities. With the financial support of the Oakville municipality and the Solicitor General of Canada, the Halton Police initiated in the summer of 1989 a program called PEACE, or Police Ethnic And Cultural Education. Under the program, nineteen high school students were selected by the

99

police department to learn about police work. They belonged to visible and cultural minorities. They were paid hourly wages and went from one unit to another. According to the Vancouver Police Department's *Annual Report* (1989), Community Relations received funding from the Secretary of State to run a Summer Youth Employment Program for young men and women from visible minority communities. It provided opportunities for such interested youths to choose "police work as a future career."

The Canadian police, in the attempt to remedy discrimination against the aboriginal peoples, have implemented a number of changes which include establishing aboriginal police programs, consultative committees, outreach advice and referral centers (King, 1997). Similar to other minorities, aboriginals have been over represented in the criminal justice process of Canada. This over representation has been combated by the following methods: 1) establishing of cultural awareness programs for police officers; 2) information programs concerning the legal structure and rights for Aboriginal peoples; 3) policing initiatives such as the Aboriginal Constable program; and 4) Tribal policing programs (Harding, Personal Conversation, 1991). The goal of the preceding programs is "to initiate, develop, and evaluate a practical and culturally sensitive policing service for Aboriginal Canadians delivered in a manner which is acceptable to them" (RCMP 1994). Stenning (1991) says that the Canadian police have publicly committed themselves to racial fairness.

Summary of multicultural and multiracial policy

(1) Multiculturalism, which is an avowed policy of the national government as incorporated in the *Charter of Rights and Freedoms* and the *Canadian Multicultural Act, 1987*, can be traced to the historical *Canadian British North American Act of 1867*. This Act legitimizes group particularism by recognizing the unique language and cultural rights of two Canadian charter groups, the English and the French. The spirit of the Canadian

Federal Union embodies the cultural duality of Canada which has been expanded to include the mosaic ideology embracing all ethnic groups including the aboriginal communities who have been encouraged to develop the goals of self-determination and self-sufficiency.

(2) The Canadian provinces have multiple multicultural initiatives and safeguards including special legislations, cabinet committees and innovative policies.

(3) The Federation of Canadian Municipalities is committed to the policy of improving race relations in Canada's municipalities.

(4) The Canadian Association of the Chiefs of Police has been financially supporting the activities of the National Multicultural Liaison Standing Committee. The Canadian Multicultural Committee that advises the Secretary of State has a police member. The RCMP has a National Advisory Committee to increase the presence of the visible minority in policing.

(5) In Ontario the Police Development and Coordination Branch of the Ministry of the Solicitor General arranges cross-cultural and race relations training. Various police departments including the Toronto Metropolitan Police Department, Vancouver Police Department and other departments have strong initiatives to improve multicultural awareness in the police including Aboriginal Police Programs.

Review of the literature

The minority position in society

Having discussed the official policies of the Canadian governments, the federal and the state, as well as the announced police policies toward the minority communities in Canada it will be useful to explore their position in society and their treatment by the police as recorded in the literature.

Fleras et al (1989) claim that, in contrast to other ethnic groups, visible minority respondents such as blacks and Chinese seem to be more aggrieved. In Canada "the defining factor of a visible minority is color, sometimes together with a dress standard dictated by creed" (*Police Notes, Canadian Police College Journal*, 1990). In a survey conducted in Toronto among "the Anglo-Saxons, the principal gate keepers of power with 45 percent of the city's population" (Samuel, 1988), they were asked "what ethnic groups, if any, are more subject to prejudice and discrimination than others." More than 65 percent of the respondents mentioned South Asians, 44 percent said Blacks, and 18 percent, Chinese.

According to Jam (1988), visible minorities "comprise close to two million people or approximately 7 percent of the country's population." They comprise 4.5 percent of the country's labor force. Identifying nine groups of visible minority, Jam lists the "Chinese, Black, Indo-Pakistani, West Asian or Arab, Filipino, Japanese, Southeast Asian, Korean and Oceanic." They are almost exclusively concentrated in the major cities (Samuel, 1988): Vancouver (14.5 percent), Toronto (13.5 percent), Calgary (8.9 percent), Edmonton (7.7 percent), and Winnipeg (6.6 percent). According to police statistics, 205,000 visible minority members reside in Vancouver; they are Chinese (100,000), Indo-Canadian *(45,000),* Japanese (12,000), Filipino (13,000), Latin American (9,000), Vietnamese (6,000), Korean (7,000), Blacks (3,200) and Native (10,000).

Richmond (1990) states that the term "visible minority" in Canada means "much the same as the term 'ethnic minority' in Britain." These terms "exclude other immigrant groups and indigenous minorities defined in terms of birthplace, language, religion or culture." He adds that the term, visible minority, has been "adopted precisely because racism is a reality in Canada (as in other countries)." Henry and Tator (1985) who claim that racism has been "an integral part of both the policies and practices of Canadian government since the beginning of this country's history," specifically mention "the treatment of Japanese Canadians in World War II," and "personal experiences with racism" by visible minority communities. Weinfeld (1989) states that the government's current role as "a firm proponent of equal opportunity for all citizens regardless of ethnic or racial origin can't conceal the historical record" which includes "blatant discrimination against Orientals," and "the disgraceful evacuation of the Japanese." Tapperman (1977) explains that "respectable middle-class" Asian immigrants were denied "civil liberties." Loree (1989) claims that the increase in the number of visible minority population in Montreal, Vancouver, and Toronto has made the general population intensely conscious of the minority issue. This experience has been strengthened by the current political climate, the *Charter of Rights of 1981*, and incidents involving minority members.

Weinfeld (1985) claims that the mosaic metaphor may be "overstated" and that the ethnic patterns in Canada and America are "more similar than the contrasting images of mosaic and melting pot would suggest." Winks (1971) identifies "the basic Canadian dilemma" of blacks in Canada who "wanted nothing more than to assimilate," but the Canadian society "did not value assimilation." Indeed, this society "persistently denied that there was a cultural norm against which assimilation could be measured," and "the black tile in the mosaic appeared ready to test the pattern." McClain (1979) argues that Canadians like to "view themselves as non-racists, and hence, discrimination tends to be extremely subtle."

The children of minority groups are placed in "special education classes or streamed into lower level academic programs," and "educators expect less from non-white children." It should be recognized that, "educators can directly contribute to racism by their own biased attitudes, assumptions and behavior" (Henry and Tator, 1985). Minorities fear that 'the opportunities for upward mobility are far less for the recent immigrants with a low educational background," because "formal education" is a prerequisite in Canada for "advancement in occupational structure" (Abu-Laban, 1980).

Their socio-economic status unites the minorities. In Canada, like elsewhere, "racial prejudice and discrimination against visible minorities are major obstacles to their achievement of economic and social integration." Samuel (1988) mentions that the level of income of Vismins (Visible minorities) "was marginally lower than that of non-vismins." Skin pigment often becomes the criterion for denying equality of opportunity to a wave of migrants "in their own or their parents' land." Discrimination in employment is a major impediment faced by the minorities. According to Ramcharan (1982), anti-discriminatory laws do not "protect their interests in the vital area of employment." Henry and Tator (1985) indicate that discrimination in the work place may be "perhaps the single most serious problem confronting visible minorities in Canada today." They are victims of employers who "wish to maintain a white work force" and to sustain the biases which are built into hiring.

The minority and the police

The Race Relations and Policing Task Force (1989) reported that native people who are not regarded as a visible minority "described treatment of them by police in much the same terms as did most visible minorities." They were "unwavering in the message that native peoples do not believe that they are fairly policed." The *Race Relations and Policing Task Force Report* (1989) expresses "concern about the current state of race relations and policing." Referring to the people who appeared before the Task Force, the report states:

> They presented with reason and passion, with commitment and tears. They convinced this Task Force of their desire to share ownership in the slogan, "our cops are tops." They also convinced us that the visible minority communities do not believe that they are policed in the same manner as the main stream, white community. They do not believe that they are policed fairly and they made a strong case for their view which cannot be ignored.

The Task Force felt that "the public submissions" definitely substantiate "a qualified indictment of the present state of race relations and policing. According to them, the "government, police and community will ignore these public reproofs and suggested remedies at our great peril." They also "clearly and unequivocally" note that "relations between police and visible minorities in the province of Ontario are at a dangerously low level."

Linden (1989) claims that "tensions exist between the police and some visible minority groups" and that "there are no easy solutions," because "a great deal of work will be required to ease these strains." Some say that it is almost a miracle that "Canada has managed to avoid large-scale interracial conflicts such as that experienced in Great Britain and the United States" (Henry and Tator, 1985).

Loree (1985) states that "despite pressures for assimilation of multiculturalism into police selecting procedures," the "discourteous treatment of the black applicants" continues. In policing, the difficulty in career advancement is another problem. *The Report of the Race Relations and Policing Task Force* (1989) states that only "one member of a visible minority" was promoted to a senior position. That single promotion caused concern to other visible minority officers and "to those in the visible minority community who feel themselves as unwelcome in policing."

In England, as Lamber (1984) recounts, "saturation policing in high crime areas" created "a widening gap" between the police and the ethnic communities." Contributing to this gap were the "racist abuse of black people by the police, a failure to protect black people" and "police harassment of the social life of black people by raiding allegedly illegal drinking clubs" (Gordon, 1983). In Canada there are complaints of harassment as the police raid bars mainly patronized by lower class ethnic patrons in cities like Vancouver. Lee (1981) states:

> Any category of citizens who lack power in major institutions of their society (institutions in the economy, polity, education, media, etc.) are liable to become police property. At one time or another, such diverse categories... as winos, hobos, unemployed drifters, labor union organizers, Japanese, blacks, long-haired youth, and homosexuals have been appropriated by the police as their property; that is, categories of people over whom the police successfully exert superior power.

105

Allegedly there is "a crisis of confidence among the minorities in the ability of the police to protect their interests" (Ramcharan, 1982). "Complaints of police brutality" are rather frequent among the black and East Indian communities, and Ramcharan feels, "cooperative intergroup relations" are being threatened by doubts about the fairness and impartiality of the legal system. Stasiulis (1989) reports that in Canada "the most common complaint" of racial minorities like the South Asians against the Metropolitan Toronto Police is police failure to "provide adequate responses to racial attacks made on community members." In England there is "the allegation on the part of the ethnic minorities that the police do not take seriously enough the existence of racial attacks" (Willis, 1985).

According to a Canadian scholar (Normandeau, 1990), it is likely that some migrants with negative attitudes toward the police are from "totalitarian countries" with the memories of "savage police and military suppression". It is also likely that "their children adopt this negative image." Although Zamble and Annesley (1987) admit that their "sample was not entirely representative of the Canadian population," they found that residents in small cities in Canada had "significantly more favorable attitudes toward the police than residents of a larger city." That the visible minorities live mostly in large cities may have something to do with their attitudes toward the police.

Summary of the review of the literature

(1) Racial prejudice and maltreatment of the ethnic groups which are historical continue till today and the visible minorities are the worst victims of racial prejudice.

(2) Racial discrimination in Canada is subtle as Canadians like to be known as non-racists.

(3) Discrimination has tainted every aspect of life: educational opportunities, economic achievement, employment and workplace.

(4) Complaints of unequal treatment, discourteous attitude, brutality and

abuse, failure to provide protection etc are constantly leveled against the police by minority groups and individuals.

(5) Minority employees complain against lack of promotion and there are also complaints of discourteous treatment of candidates of ethnic origins by police departments.

Police officers on multiculturalism
Responses analyzed from questionnaires

Questionnaires were distributed to police officers through their departments in Montreal, Ottawa and Toronto. On the basis of the responses, the information gathered was as follows:

Montreal: In Montreal 82 percent of officers indicated that the lack of empathy with Canadian culture and reluctance of integration had made the visible minorities indifferent to Canadian tradition. Minorities suffered from a lack of belonging to the country where they had migrated. Their value system was different. In some cases their sense of difference with the mainstream culture was so marked that the feeling of isolation from society was acute. This feeling of isolation made ethnic minorities flock together, making them further isolated.

These problems, particularly the lack of integration with the larger society, generated socio-economic disadvantages for them and gave rise to criminality. As a result, society generally became reluctant to recognize the minorities as useful. The lack of acceptance led to discrimination in education, employment, and housing. With an absence of education and the related disadvantages, the minorities did not have judges and attorneys, and their members did not occupy other important positions in the legal system. Although they did not suffer from a lack of due process in Montreal or other big cities in Canada, their position was more vulnerable in the system of justice as a result of non-representation. Minorities had trouble understanding the law.

Their unique predicament encouraged racial and cultural prejudices. Denied equal opportunities in education and employment, some minorities, particularly the Jamaicans, unlike the Chinese and the Vietnamese, began living on welfare. These people gradually shifted to the periphery of the mainstream society, even abandoning such basic responsibilities as parenting their children in the Canadian way. They jeopardized the prospects of future generations by refusing to keep track of their children and neglecting their upbringing.

Ottawa: In Ottawa 54 percent of the officers maintained that the visible minorities were affected unfavorably by socio-cultural differences that existed between them and the Canadians belonging to the mainstream. As a result, they were less affluent and had experienced many barriers to integration. Their inability to acquire proficiency in the languages strengthened the walls of isolation. Minorities who failed to identify and assimilate into the Canadian way of life often had financial problems, were unable to take advantage of travel and housing opportunities. In addition, the failure of minority integration, regardless of the minorities' race, led to minorities being vulnerable to inferiority complexes and fear psychoses.

Police respondents traced the disadvantages of the minorities to several causes which included: poor language skills, unfamiliarity with the Canadian laws, bigotry and racism of the white, and to the minorities' inability to assimilate into Canadian culture. Minorities were alienated because of cultural value conflicts. They were frustrated because they did not belong to the world in which they worked; its values were not understood and, as a result, they formed their own groups with ethnic leaders, some of whom were trouble-makers and radical in their behavior. The migrants who failed to integrate into the new culture were unable to take advantage of the generous opportunities in the areas of schooling, housing, food-programs, and employment.

Explaining the advantages of integration, respondents stated that some groups like the Vietnamese successfully embraced Canadian cultural values, including work ethics, and prospered. They were able to overcome many disadvantages that those who failed to integrate were unable to achieve. The integrated Vietnamese showed that it was not unusual for all migrants to suffer initially, as they learned to adjust their life styles and values to the culture of a new society. Vietnamese who had language problems eventually succeeded in integrating into society.

Ignorance prevented them from internalizing the Canadian laws. The respondents maintained that, because integration was lacking, minorities did not attempt to secure government protection. The minorities' own Mafia's victimized them, and minority victims suffered acts of lawlessness in silence instead of informing the police. The lack of understanding of Canadian police culture was an important reason for the minorities' failure to report crimes to the police. They were afraid of complaining to the police authorities, because they feared police harassment. They had inaccurate perceptions of Canadian police culture. They were unable to understand Canadian legal provisions like wife beating.

The French-speaking population is unfriendly to the police because of English and the French conflict occurring between Quebec and Toronto. In Ottawa it is not unusual for French-speaking drivers from Quebec to tell the police, "You have stopped me because I am from Quebec." Similar complaints are heard from blacks who claim they are stopped by the police, because they are blacks. Also, Chinese make the same charge.

Toronto: In Toronto all respondents attributed the difficulties of minorities to their lack of an understanding of Canadian society, an overall lack of understanding of Canadian culture and what appeared like minorities' indifference to the Canadian way of life. Immigrants to Canada might be reluctant to embrace the dominant Canadian culture because of misunderstanding of the implications of multiculturalism. Minority difficulties often arose because of their inability to understand that Canada was basically an English-speaking country with a predominant Western culture. Multiculturalism on the part of Canadian society did not mean that minorities should not be assimilated into Canadian society. Those who do not understand what multiculturalism should mean experience a shocking hiatus between what they considered to be reality and official theory. Multiculturalism requires assimilation of the minority into the culture of the majority. Minority immigrants who do not grasp the assimilation aspects of multiculturalism are at a disadvantage. Schools located in minority neighborhood were inferior to schools in white neighborhoods. Minority students were directed towards vocational education programs. Many minority members, according to police officers, applied for welfare and this compounded their problems since welfare allowances deprived them of the motivation for seeking employment.

Since minorities did not understand Canadian laws, particularly traffic laws, and this was often a cause for legal troubles. The minorities coming from the Third World countries either did not understand or paid little attention to the observance of minor laws including traffic laws but they were careful about laws concerning major crimes. A result of legal difficulties was that the mutual respect between the police and minorities was nonexistent. Owing to their adherence to the culture of their native lands, some minorities did not view policing as an honorable occupation. They were afraid of the police, because they remembered unflattering images of the police in their native countries. Oriental groups were especially afraid of telling the police about offensive acts like intimidation and assault, committed by their own people. Vietnamese and Chinese always attempted to be secretive with the police.

Conversations in patrol cars with police officers

The observer author made trips to Montreal, Toronto, Ottawa, Oakville as well as Vancouver to visit minority neighborhoods with police officers, and talk to them as well as to police executives about various relevant issues, particularly, regarding police views, perceptions, experiences and knowledge about the minority groups they confront in every day work.

In Toronto, Montreal, Oakville, and Ottawa officers were of the opinion that Canadian society displayed racial and cultural prejudices against minorities. One sergeant in Ottawa observed that the visible minorities had to fight white bigotry and racism. There was a lack of respect for degrees earned in some foreign countries which hurt some ethnic groups. They also had fewer opportunities for education. They failed to acquire professional skills because of prejudice against them. Language was considered to be a major problem for minorities. Two officers from the Race Relations Unit in Toronto said that their foreign accents were a cause of prejudice against some minority members. A police director in Montreal (Personal Conversation, John Dalzell, 1989) said that many immigrants to Quebec felt disoriented when they arrived in Montreal, because they thought Canada was an English-speaking country. He referred to the Bill 178 which required immigrants to send their children to French schools. Although only 20 percent of children in French schools were migrants in 1985, the number increased to 80 percent in 1988. Learning French was confusing for the children and frustrating for their parents. Bilingualism was clearly a challenge for immigrants from English-speaking countries. They also found it difficult to adopt bilingualism (Stenning, 1991).

Socio-economic disadvantages of minority groups, the police felt, were caused by callousness in society. Such groups, particularly those migrating from poorer societies of the world, suffered more economic hardships. One Ottawa police officer who had migrated from the West Indies mentioned that a lack of and understanding of Canadian culture was considered a handicap in the job market. Foreigners also were paid less than others. One staff inspector in Ottawa who had migrated across the Atlantic felt that minorities did not have access to quality life. Certain jobs like policing were not open to them. One sergeant with a German background endorsed the views of the staff inspector; minority members had to work harder than others to prove themselves. He added that these problems

111

affecting minority groups were more in evidence outside Ottawa where levels of education of the inhabitants precluded racial and ethnic discrimination. In Montreal police officers knew of factories where minority women worked sewing garments at lower hourly rates than the minimum wage.

The observer author noted that, while moving through the areas of public housing complexes in Toronto, Montreal and Ottawa, patrol officers discussed the young people of minority communities hanging around street corners. The youngsters' rough manners and attitude were resented by the patrol officers. The police complained that minority parents did not exercise control over their children. One officer said that women from countries like Pakistan suffered more since, compared to men in those countries, women were less educated and consequently had less skill in English. A Toronto police officer mentioned to the observer author that individuals from some countries retained their misconceived notions concerning class and status which made them incapable of understanding the egalitarian Western system.

In conversations with police officers in the patrol cars the observer author was shown that Toronto's Police District 31, the Metro Housing area, was the home of thousands of residents of all races and cultures, including minority migrants from the Caribbean Islands, Ecuador, Mexico and Colombia. An officer expressed a sigh of relief that Vietnamese, Chinese and Koreans, who he considered to be more enterprising, did not live in the Housing Project now. This contributed to the lessening of tension in this potentially explosive neighborhood. The patrol officers in Toronto constantly returned to the theme that cosmopolitanism had its price, and they seemed to echo Banton (1964) who commented that "a heterogeneous population" in America was less "tractable" than the population in a "region of greater social stability." In Toronto's South and North Regent Park, an area with subsidized housing, clashes occurred between white and black youths. Both groups seemed to be intolerant of each other. On Eglington Avenue, Jamaicans, Portuguese, and Italians represented different cultures. In St. Dennis one saw Southeast Asians and Indians of African origin. In the East York area there was a predominantly white population. The Greeks dominated Southern Danforth Avenue, and the Portuguese had concentrated in Dovercourt Road. The Village of Parkdale, where people from Nova Scotia had lived, was populated by some yuppies and Vietnamese. On Landsdowne Avenue there lived a cosmopolitan population of Portuguese, Ukrainians, Indians, and immigrants from the West Indies. Vietnamese, Chinese, and Filipinos lived on Dundas Street, and Vietnamese and Chinese were predominant on Bathurst Street. An Oriental influence was noticeable in Spadina. The Kensington market had been Italian but was now dominated by Portuguese. Argentinean restaurants were located on College Street. Italians, Portuguese, and Vietnamese lived in Little Italy. Bloor Street had a mixed population of blacks, Asians and whites. On Spadina Street a native Canadian Center and native apartments had been built. On Dupont Street there were blacks, Hispanics, Portuguese, and whites.

Officers said that assaults, drug abuse and thefts occurred in these ethnic pockets in Toronto. In the opinion of one retired police commander in Toronto, ethnic crimes involved more blacks, some of whom were violent and frightening. According to one sergeant, undesirable behavior, including domestic disputes and drunkenness, was reported from the Metro Housing area. A senior commander in Ottawa remarked that several successful prosecutions of extortion cases had helped create for some minorities a degree of confidence in the police. However, even when victimization of minorities by members of their ethnic groups became known to the police, they were unable to arrest the miscreants because the victims often would not cooperate.

Difficulties experienced by minorities within the legal system were considerable. Minorities perceived that they suffered from the lack of due process. They complained that the police failed to differentiate between law-abiding and law-breaking members of their communities. The police resented that members of visible minority groups did not understand the legal implications of some acts like wife beating. One Ottawa constable said that a Chinese colleague resented having to work in Somerset Street, because he had to deal with other Chinese who did not welcome him as one of their own. According to a Toronto police officer with nineteen years of experience, the lack of understanding between the police and the minorities was mutual. This lack of understanding can make minorities averse to accepting a member of their community as a police officer.

There were police officers who also resented the Chinese and the Italians who were concentrated in ethnic neighborhoods. Chinese and Italians minorities were more concentrated in certain pockets in Montreal and Toronto. In Vancouver the largest groups of settlers were Chinese, Indo-Canadians, Japanese, Filipinos, and people from English-speaking regions. Another minority group that the police must deal with are the aboriginal Indian people, who are descendents from the original people of Canada. In the past several decades aboriginal peoples have been involved in numerous acts of agitation with regards to land-claim protests, environmental issues, ranging from fishing rights to deforestation and road developments.

Some police officers, particularly in Ottawa, were critical regarding the department's role in promoting minority or cultural awareness. Many of them had enjoyed the cultural awareness seminar that the department required. One experienced foot-constable in Ottawa mentioned that several years back a few command-level officers had a negative attitude towards minorities, but it had ended.

Summary of police officers' views

The views of police officers expressed through the questionnaires and conversations can be broadly summarized as follows:

(1) Minority groups show an incapacity to integrate with the majority community, which drives them to the periphery of the society causing them to suffer from economic hardships, exposure to criminality and

other consequences that befall marginal groups.

(2) Such characteristics of marginality, the attributes of existence in the periphery of the society, cause the minority groups to lose respect from the majority community which perpetuates their inferior status.

(3) Minority groups demonstrate a lack of knowledge of law, and the inability to understand the implications of such behaviors as wife beating, irresponsible parenting, not reporting crimes and distrust of the police,

(4) There are a variety of crimes in the minority pockets of the major urban centers such as thefts, assaults, drugs, and also mafia activities, but the police are unable to handle them successfully because of the lack of cooperation as mentioned in (3) above.

Discussions and recommendations

Canada has strong laws, policies, initiatives and a commitment to racial harmony, equality of treatment for all people irrespective of race, class or vulnerability to any other form of prejudicial distinction. However, the review of the literature and the views of the officers incorporated above demonstrate clearly that Canadian society and the police have a long way to go to achieve the state of racial justice and fairness as ambitiously propounded in the laws, policies and other official sources.

True, the police are changing their "perception and style" (Fleras et al, 1989) and making a transition to multicultural policing and are becoming aware that "blacks will increase ... Asians and other racial/ethnic minorities will increase even faster in this "culturally heterogeneous society" (McDougall, 1988). However, there exist need for a great deal of caution and retrospection. In calling for "adapting our justice system to the cultural needs of Canada's North," Morrow (1981) refers to the need for national tolerance toward minorities. He says that "it is for all Canadians to ensure that these fine people — both Indian and Eskimo —

and their aspirations...are met halfway; that they be treated as equal citizens."
There is much to learn, "the policing community in Canada should prepare itself"
(Ogle, 1991) to deal with visible minorities. In a Final Report submitted to the
Metropolitan Toronto Police Services Board, a consulting firm (1982) suggested
that "Metropolitan Toronto's mosaic of diverse ethnic and economic groups has
major implications for management and programming." The Chief Justice of the
High Court of Justice in Ontario claims that "simple tolerance" of the various
ethnic and cultural diversities by Canadian police is not enough. What is needed is
"an appreciation" of the differences and "a sincere effort" to understand the
diversity (Evans, 1985)

The effective practice of multiculturalism places demands on police
resources asking for renewed innovative efforts in the areas of recruitment,
training, promotional policies and police-community relations (McKenna, 1998).
Minority recruitment seems to be a very important step. Loree (1989) feels that
most officers from minority communities would welcome the opportunities their
positions offered them to serve their own people. His point of view seemed very
reasonable to the observer author as he observed a Toronto police officer of East
Indian origin interacting with tradesmen from India. A genuine rapport existed
between the officer and the members of the Indian community; they seemed to
enjoy their interactions very much. An officer in Ottawa mentioned that the
department's performance evaluation system took into account only the statistics
of arrests, fines, and computer checks on vehicles. No motivation existed for
officers to spend time on community relations. Multiculturalism policy, if it is
enforced diligently, should help departments to change police performance
appraisal systems. Speaking of the situation in England, Rex (1984) says "the
present generation" of British police inspectors seems to "have an archaic,
colonialist, racist and authoritarian attitude." These attitudes probably "gained
their promotion," because, Rex feels, "tough-mindedness is far more likely to lead
to promotion than refined sensibility towards ethnic minorities." An Ottawa patrol

116

officer echoed similar sentiments indicating that a respectful attitude towards multiculturalism did not earn promotions and it was not presented as a policy to be seriously practiced.

An officer from Toronto mentioned to the observer author that he had not received any message — in terms of the core mission (Schein, 1986) — from the department that ethnic relations were to be given special importance. Further, this officer felt that a lack of fairness existed in the department in its treatment of officers, and consequently it was not realistic for the department to expect personnel to be fair toward visible minorities. A positive understanding of police and minority relations can be achieved if there is discussion regarding the department's policies and thinking between management and street cops (Reuss-Ianni and Ianni, 1979). Ideally management's public goals and policy objectives concerning minorities should be endorsed by the rank-and-file. Police officers in general should understand both the official Canadian policy and the public position of the police. As Desroches and Fleras (1985) state, "immigration and ethnicity in Canada involve many complex issues." They explain:

> By gaining some appreciation for Canadian immigration history, government policy, as well as the contributions and adjustments made by minority community members, police officers will bring a heightened understanding to situations they may encounter in the enforcement of law and order.

It was pointed out by patrol officers, as the observer author moved with them, that there was the need of the political and administrative will to improve the lives of the minority people. The police realized that improving public housing could also pay rich dividends and pointed out to the observer author that an unofficial brothel had stood on 169 Clarence Street where hookers took their clients. When the building was renovated, the prostitutes left, and conditions improved. Many officers wished that the same energetic renovations could be made to improve living conditions in the housing projects. As a result of the realization of the implications of the "Broken Window" theory (Wilson and

Kelling, 1982), the Ottawa municipality renovated the Debra Avenue area where the quality of life had improved. The housing projects on the South side of the city were also improving, and calls to the police had decreased. Another officer mentioned that the collection of garbage in the housing project had improved; as a result, the discipline and orderliness in the projects also improved. In Lower Town patrol officers were happy to say that following improved street lighting, the cleaning of shabby areas, and other renovations, people in this area experienced a sense of safety and security. Drunks and other undesirables were no longer found there.

Brown (1982) has enumerated the reasons for local police success in England's Handsworth District which had a growing "concern...about relationships between police and black youth." He attributes policing success in this "multi-racial urban context" to a "notable model of policing by consent," based on "the backing and active support of the great majority of local people." The police worked despite "growing, and extremely adverse, social/economic and militant political pressures." They recognized the fact that "policing by consent is a continuous process of interaction and reciprocation." Their work was activated by "a community-based approach to policing," and it was rooted in "complementary aspects of an overall plan to tackle both symptoms and causes of crime and disorder." In Flint, Michigan, Trojanowicz (1986) comments that "the foot patrol interaction of white officers in black communities and black officers in white communities" had a benign impact on "a very serious racial problem" in that city. The need is "to focus on the quality of relationship between the community and the department" (Groves et al, 1980). In their study to guide the Metro Dade Police Department make "policy decisions" based on the "understanding of the complexities involved in this dynamic, multi-ethnic community," Alpert and Dunham (1988) report that among all ethnic groups there is "considerable citizen support for individualized community policing style." However, the police in different neighborhoods do not practice "differing styles of policing to match the unique characteristics of the neighborhoods." In order to implement custom-made styles of policing, they suggest police training to be specifically designed for a district which should include "knowledge concerning unique characteristics of the neighborhoods." They suggest a style of policing "most appropriate and effective" for a particular neighborhood taking into consideration "specific consumer demands and priorities." They ask for "a total commitment to neighborhood intervention and community evaluation."

In *Commission des Droits de la Personnel du Quebec* (1988) it has been stated that the most frequent complaint of ethnic groups is their "certain inability to communicate properly with the police force" because of "the image of the police as being inaccessible." Among the suggestions made was a need for the expansion of the "direct channels of communication between the police and cultural communities." The Chief of Canada's Human Rights Commission (Yalden, 1989) believes in a need to "better attune our police officers to the multicultural and multiracial communities in which we live." He also admits that the Royal Canadian Mounted Police, the Canadian Association of the Chiefs of Police, the Canadian Police College, and the Canadian Police Association are "making such efforts." They have an important relationship with the visible minorities. Multiculturalism is likely to keep police officers generally aware of visible minorities which may help police understand that "many offenses, particularly intimate violence will not be reported to them unless there is trust of police competence and impartiality" (Yarmey, 1991).

Canadian police have been emphasizing community policing. Lewis writes that, "For community policing to succeed, there must be a considerable reorientation of the philosophy and operational priorities of police forces" (1993). Lewis further claims that police officers should be de-emphasizing their role as primarily law enforcement officers. The emphasis on the law enforcement role encourages officers to view all citizens as criminals or potential criminals. Police have to recognize that community policing is intelligent policing allowing the officer to be proactive in crime solving (Lewis, 1993). LaPrairie (1988) mentioned that in Canadian Indian reserves "the native police are called upon to fulfill a variety of social service and crisis intervention roles." The demand for a "range of broadly based social service roles" performed by the native police is "much broader than that of the Royal Canadian Mounted Police in nonnative communities." In his account of the Canadian experience of policing native Indians, Griffiths (1988) suggests that "policing programs must address the unique policing requirements of individual native communities and reserves." He (1982) also found "increasing positive police-youth interaction and a more favorable view of the police by adolescents." Any kind of human ties, links and affinities with a community seems to inspire confidence in the police which results in increasing requests for police involvement in the everyday life of people. In Vancouver, the Police Department required officers to attend community meetings, organize games for local youths, participate in social events, and get involved in the life of the community. According to Sergeant Robert Murphy (Personal Conversation, 1991), calls for community involvement became so numerous that the police were unable to handle them.

Conclusion

Goldstein (1977) says that police leaders must be thinkers. More importantly every police officer must be a thinker and develop insights into the predicaments of the people whom he serves (Das, 1987). When thinking police officers serve as patrol officers, detectives, and police executives, as thinking individuals they will no doubt be in a better position to develop empathy towards all people including the members of the visible minority community in Canada. A thinking officer should also be able to appreciate that the "Police in a plural society" (Loree, 1985) are likely to find themselves "marginal in the dynamic processes involved in a multiracial and multicultural milieu by virtue of their generally conservative stance with respect to social change." The literature does depict police officers as conservative and conformity-minded and this discussion has not changed over the years (McNamara, 1967; Boswden, 1978: Das, 1990). Willis (1985) also reveals that 30 percent of the English police respondents who agreed with the statement that "when it comes to the things that count most, all races are certainly not equal" believed that England did not need to apprehend race riots displaying their insensitivity to the actual feeling of the minorities before the riots erupted. Sewell (1985) maintains that successful police reform demands that "the police are in tune with current social values." Unless they are able to develop sensitivity to people, their aspirations and the changes in the environment, they will find themselves "helpless to overcome many of the problems thrust on them by our changing society" (Kelly and Kelly, 1976).

However, the police in Canada like the police everywhere are also required to administer the laws and regulations, control behavior and prevent disorder from any individual or groups. As *The Report of the Race Relations and Policing Task Force* (1989) states, being "the main agents of social control in a democratic society," the police must be "strong, assertive, and, to some degree authoritarian." They have to act as "guardians of symbolic order ... the coercive arm of the state" (Ericson, 1989). In this role it is inevitable that the police will fail to please all people at all times, incur wrath at times, and attract criticism from some quarters or the other when they strong position to enforce the law or maintain order.

Like other institutions the police are also subject to the developments in society which may constrain or facilitate their strategies. It is noted, for example, that more minorities are being sought for hiring by police agencies in Canada. But it is also to be borne in mind that "one is unlikely to find a police force that mirrors its plural society, so one is unlikely to find a representative bureaucracy" (Enloe, 1980). In the absence of real political powers, minority protection legislation is often perfunctory. Eisinger (1983) recalls that in spite of the *1972 Equal Employment Opportunity Act* in America, the hiring of minorities was not

121

important on the agenda of the city governments until the election of the black mayors who "have not waited for black applicants to appear on their doorsteps but have initiated active recruitment searches." In 1975 sixteen American cities "averaging more than one-third in black population" had white mayors, and blacks were severely "under-represented in local government levels, particularly at the managerial level." It was not until blacks became mayors, that "black public sector employment has been a focus of affirmative action efforts." Eisinger notes that increases in police employment of blacks were "dramatic" in the 1970s in Detroit, Newark, and Washington, D.C. Although, as MacDonald and Humphrey (1979) comment that, in case such laws as the comprehensive human rights codes, "are not effectively enforced" they will "constitute a sham." It is not totally in the hands of the police to eliminate discrimination, prejudice and injustice from society. Fletcher (Quoted in *The Report of Race Relations and Policing Task Force, 1989* notes that "racist attitudes are represented in Canadian police force to the degree that they are present in society as a whole." There is the need for concerted action among legislators, administrators, police leaders and others.

Experiences from other countries will help Canadian police develop a balanced perspective on the minority and police issues. One senior commander of the Toronto Metropolitan Police Department resented, as he talked to the observer author, that visible minorities were misdirected by a few so-called leaders. He added that these so-called leaders were hungry for political powers, and they exploited the minorities to obtain favors from politicians at municipal, state, and national levels. A similar situation has been reported from the United Kingdom. In deprived ghettos of England, young West Indians are concerned with "the politics of resistance...how they prepare to defend themselves on the street against the police" (Rex, 1984). They seem to want "confrontation," and perhaps "the black political leadership ... do not want any change in policing policy because confrontation is what they most need, to advance their kind of political cause."

Problems between minorities and criminal justice systems including the police exist all over the world (Skolnick, 1966; Alex, 1969; Gronfors, 1981; Hagan and Albonetti, 1982; Petersilia, 1983; Zatzz, 1987; Junger 1989; Hyder, 1990; Spohn and Cederblom, 1991). In the context of the American situation in this regard, it is said that "blacks, lower-class members, and the uneducated" are likely to face "some form of discriminatory treatment ... unequal justice" in every phase—arrest, conviction, and sentencing—in the criminal justice process (Flowers, 1988). As Willis (1985) writes, until 1981 Britain "assumed rather arrogantly" that race riots in the United States and elsewhere "were the result of extremes of racial inequality the likes of which would never been seen" in that country.

Experiences and apprehensions in different parts of the world should serve as the reminder that it is certainly worthwhile for the police in Canada, as well as in other countries, that in the area of minority relations, police are confronted with two major challenges. One concerns their own occupational failing in their tendency to look upon minorities as marginal people. Second, the minority community demands that they must be policed as fairly and as justly as the majority community. Their universal complaint that they do not receive that level of police service should be taken seriously.

References

Abu-Laban. Baba. 1980. *An Olive Branch on the Family Tree.* Toronto: McClelland and Stewart.

Alex, Nicholas. 1969. *Black in Blue. A Study of Negro Policemen.* New York: Appleton Century-Crofts.

Alpert, Geoffrey P. and Roger G. Dunham. 1988. *Policing Multi-Ethnic Neighborhoods.* Westport, CT: Greenwood Press.

Banton, Michael. 1964. *The Policeman in the Community.* New York: Basic Books.

Bourget, M. Ronald. 1987. Personal Interview. Montreal.

Bowden, T. 1978. *Beyond the Limits of Law.* England: Harmondsworth.

Brown, Craig. 1969. Introduction. In Ramsey Cook, Craig Brown, and Carl Berger, eds. *Minorities, Schools, and Politics.* Toronto: University of Toronto Press.

Brown, John. 1982. *Policing by Multi-Racial Consent.* London: Bedford Square Press.

The Canadian Multiculturalism Act. 1988.

Commission des Droits de la Personne du Quebec. 1988. *Excerpts from Final Report.* Quebec: Ministry of Communications.

Daizell, John. 1989. Personal Interview. Montreal.

Das, Dilip K. 1987. *Understanding Police Human Relations.* Metuchen, NJ: The Scarecrow Press.

Desroches, Frederick J. and Angie Fleras. 1985. Immigration and Ethnicity in Canada. In Brian K. Cryderman, ed. *Police and Ethnicity.* Toronto: Butterworth & Co.

Eisinger, Peter K. 1983. Black Mayors and the Politics of Racial Economic Advancement. In William McCready, ed. *Culture, Ethnicity, and Identity.* New York: Academic Press.

Enloe, Cynthia H. 1980. *Police, Military and Ethnicity: Foundations of State Power*. New Brunswick, NJ. Transaction Books.

Ericson, Richard V. 1989. Patrolling the Facts: Secrecy and Publicity in Police Work. *The British Journal of Sociology.* 40 (2), 205-226.

Essed, Philomena. 1991. *Understanding Everyday Racism*. Newbury Park, CA: Sage Publications.

Evens, Gregory T. 1985. Forword. In Brian K. Cryderman, ed. *Police, Race and Ethnicity*. Toronto: Butterworth & Co.

Fleras, Augie, Frederick J. Desroches, Chris O'Toole, and George Davis. 1989. Bridging the Gap. *Canadian Police College Journal* 13 (3), 153-164.

Flowers, Ronald Barri. 1988. *Minorities and Criminality*. Westport, CT: Greenwood Press.

Frideres, James S. 1989. *Multiculturalism and Intergroup Relations*. Westport, CT: Greenwood Press.

Goldberg, Michael A. 1986. Comparisons of American and Canadian Cities. In Daniel H. Flaherty and William R. McKercher, eds. *Southern Exposure: Canadian Perspectives on the United States*. Toronto: McGraw-Hill Ryerson Ltd.

Gordon, Paul. 1983. *White Law.' Racism in the Police, Courts and Prisons*. London: Pluto Press Ltd.

Griffiths, Curt Taylor. 1988. Native Indians and the Police: The Canadian Experience. *Police Studies* 11(4), 155-160.

1982. Police School Programs: The Realities of the Remedy. *Canadian Journal of Criminology* 24 (3), 329-340.

Gronfors, Martti. 1981. Police Perception of Social Problems and Clients: The Case of Gypsies in Finland, *International Journal of the Sociology of Law* (9), 345-359.

Groves, Theodore, Thom Moore and Edward K. Reimer. 1980. An Approach to Problems in Police Community Relations. *Journal of Community Psychology* 8 (4), 357-363.

Guidon, Hubert. 1988. *Quebec Society: Tradition, Modernity, and Nationhood.* Toronto: University of Toronto Press.

Gwyn, Richard. 1980. *The Northern Magus.* Toronto: McClelland and Stewart Ltd.

Hagan, John and Celesta Albonetti. 1982. Race, Class and the Perception of Criminal Injustice in America. *American Journal of Sociology* 88 (2), 329-355.

Harding, James. 1991. Personal Interview. Toronto.

Harding, James 1991. "Policing and Aboriginal Justice," *Canadian Journal of Criminology,* Volume, 33, No. 3-4, pp. 363-383.

Henry, Frances and carol Totor. 1985. Racism in Canada: Social Myths and Strategies for Change. In Rita M. Bienvienue and Jay E. Goldstein, eds. *Ethnicity and Ethnic Relations in Canada.* Toronto: Butterworth & Co.

Hickling-Johnson Ltd. 1982. *Final report* #4 Toronto

Hyder, Ken. 1990. Cause for Complaint. *New Statesman and Society* 3 (83), 25-26.

Jam, Harish C. 1988. The Recruitment and Selection of Visible Minorities in Canadian Police Organizations, 1985-1987, Canadian Public Administration 31(4), 463-482.

Junger, Marianne. 1989. Discrepancies between Police and Self-report. Data for Dutch Racial Minorities, *The British Journal of Criminology* 29 (3), 273-284.

Kelly, William and Norma Kelly. 1976. *Policing in Canada.* Toronto: The Macmillan Company of Canada Ltd.

King, Mike, 1997. "Policing and Public Order Issues in Canada: Trends for Change," *Policing and Society,* Volume 8, pp. 47-76.

Lambert, J. L. 1984. The Policing Crisis. In Philip Norton, ed. *Law and Order and British Politics.* Hampshire, England: Gower Publishing Company.

LaPrairie, Carol Pitcher. 1988. Community Types, Crime, and Police Services on Canadian Indian Reserves. *Journal of Research in Crime and Delinquency* 25 (4), 375-391.

Lederman, W. R. 1981. *Continuing Canadian Constitutional Dilemmas.* Toronto: Butterworth & Co.

Lee, John Alan. 1981. Some Structural Aspects of Police Deviance. In Clifford D. Shearing,ed. *Organizational Police Deviance.* Toronto: Butterworth & Co.

Lewis, Clare. 1989. Personal Interview. Ottawa.

Lewis, Clare. 1993. "The Police and The Community," in *Community Policing in Canada,"* James Chacko and Stephen E. Nancoo, Editors, Toronto, Canada: Canadian Scholars' Press Inc., 269-273.

Linden, Rick. 1989. Demographic Change and the Future of Policing. In Donald J. Loree, ed. *Future Issues in Policing: Symposium Preceedings. Ottawa:* Canadian Police College.

Long, D. A. 1995. "On Violence and Healing: Aboriginal Experiences, 1960-1993," in J. I. Ross, Editor, *Violence in Canada: Socio-Political Perspective,* Don Mill, Ont.: Oxford University Press, Canada, pp.40-77.

Loree, Donald J. 1989. Personal Interview. Ottawa, 1989.

1985. Police in a Plural Society. *Canadian Police College Journal,* 9 (4) 391-412.

MacDonald, R. and John Humphrey, eds. 1979. *The Practice of Freedom.* Toronto: Butterworth & Co. Ltd.

McClain, Paula Denice. 1979. *Alienation and Resistance: The Political Behavior of Afro-Canadians.* Palo Alto, CA: R & E Research Associates, Inc.

McCready, William C. 1983 Preface. In William C. McCready, ed. *Culture, Ethnicity, and Identity.* New York: Academic Press.

McKenna, Paul F. 1998. *Policing in Canada,* Scarborough, Ontario: Prentice-Hall.

McNamara, John. 1967. Uncertainties in Police Work. In D. Bordua, ed. *The Police: Six Sociological essays.* New York: John Wiley and Sons.

127

McDougall, Allan K. 1988. *Policing. The Evolution of a Mandate.* Ottawa: Canadian Police College.

Metropolitan Toronto Police Services Board. 1990. *Race Relations Policy.* Toronto.

Miner, Michael. 1986. *Police Intercultural Training Manual.* Ottawa: Canadian Association of Chiefs of Police.

Morrow, W. G. 1981. Adapting Our Justice System to the Cultural Needs of Canada's North. In Louis A. Knafla, ed. *Crime and Criminal Justice in Europe and Canada.* Waterloo, Ontario: Wilfrid Laurier University Press.

Murphy, Robert. 1991. Personal Interview. Vancouver.

Normandeau, Andre. 1990. The Police and Ethnic Minorities. *Canadian Police College Journal* 14 (3), 2 15-229.

Ogle, Dan. 1991. *Strategic Planning for Police.* Ottawa: Ministry of Supply and Services, Canada.

Ontario Race Relations and Policing Task Force. 1989. *The Report.* Toronto.

Petersilia, J. 1983. *Racial Disparities in the Criminal Justice System.* Santa Monica, CA: Rand Corporation.

Police Notes. 1990. In *Canadian Police College Journal* 14 (3), 2 15-229.

Ramcharan, Subhas. 1982. *Racism: Non-whites in Canada.* Toronto: Butterworth & Co.

Reuss-Ianni, E. and F. A. J. Ianni. 1979. *Street Cops vs. Management Cops: The Social Oganizatin of Police Precinct.* New York: Columbia University Teachers college.

Rex, John. 1984. Law and Order in Multiracial Inner-City Areas: The Issues after Scarman, in *Law and Order and British Politics.* Hampshire, England: Gower Publishing Company.

Richmond, Anthony H. 1990. Race Relations and Immigration: A Comparative Perspective. *International Journal of Comparative Sociology* 31(3-4), 156-176.

1967, *Post-War Immigrants in Canada.* Toronto: University of Toronto Press.

Royal Canadian Mounted Police. 1994. *Fact Sheets 1994,* Ottawa, RCMP.

Samuel, T. John. 1988. The Third World Migration. A paper presented at the National Symposium on Demography of Immigrant, Racial and Ethnic Groups in Canada. Winnipeg.

Samuel, John T. and Senaka K. Suriya. 1993. "A Demographically Reflective Workforce for Canadian Police," in *Community Policing in Canada,* James Chacko and Stephen E. Nancoo, editors, Toronto, Canada: Canadian Scholars' Press Inc., 275-287.

Schein, Edward. 1985. *Organizational Culture.* San Francisco, CA: Jossey-Bass.

Sewell, John. 1985. *Police: Urban Policing in Canada.* Toronto: James Lorimer & Company.

Skolnick, Jerome H. 1966. *Justice without Trial.* New York: John Wiley and Sons.

Spohn, Cassia and Jerry Cederbiom. 1991. Race and Disparities in Sentencing: A Test of the Liberation Hypothesis. *Justice Quarterly* 8 (3), 305-327.

Stasiulis, Daiva K. 1989. Minority Resistance in the Local State: Toronto in the 1970s and 1980s. *Ethnic and Racial Studies* 12 (1), 63-83.

Stenning, Philip C. 1991. Personal Interview, Toronto.

Stewart, Gordon. 1986. *The Origins of Canadian Politics: A Comparative Approach.* Vancouver: University of British Columbia Press.

Talbot, C.K., C.H.S. Jayawardene, and T.J. Juliani. 1985. *Canada's Constable.* Ottawa: Crimcare Inc.

Tapperman, Lorne. 1977. *Crime Control.* Toronto: McGraw-Hill Ryerson Ltd.

Trojanowicz, Robert. 1987. Neighbourhood Patrol Strategies: The Flint, Michigan Experience. In Donald J. Loree and Chris Murphy, eds. *Community Policing in the 1980s: Recent Advances in Police Programs.* Ottawa: Ministry of Supply and Services.

Valpy, Michael. 1990. Is Hunting Bad Guys Good Use of Police? *The Globe and Mail.* October 31.

Vancouver Police Department. 1989. *Annual Report.*

Weinfeld, Morton. 1989. Canada's Racism Record: Some Cause for Optimism. *The Globe and Mail,* July 18, A6-A7.

1985. Myth and Reality in the Canadian Mosaic: "Affective Ethnicity". In Rita Bienvenue and Jay E. Goldstein, eds. *Ethnicity and Ethnic Relations in Canada.* Toronto: Butterworth & Co.

Willis, Carole F. *1985.* The Police and Race Relations in England. *Police Studies* 8 (4), 227-230.

Wilson, James Q. and George L. Kelling. 1982. The Police and Neighborhood Safety. *Atlantic Monthly,* March, 29-38.

Winks, Robin W. 1971. *The Blacks in Canada.* Montreal: McGill University Press.

Yaladen, Maxwell F. 1989. Presentation to the Ontario Race Relations and Policing Task Force. M*inutes, Race Relations and Policing Task Force.* Ottawa, 35-45.

Yarmey, A. Daniel. 1991. Retrospective Perceptions of Police Following Victimization. *Canadian Police College Journal 15* (2), 137-143.

Zamble, Edward and Phyllis Annesley. 1987. Some Determinants of Public Attitudes toward the Police. *Journal of Police Science and Administration 15* (4), 285-290.

Zatz, Marjorie S. 1987. The Changing Forms of Racial/Ethnic Biases in Sentencing. *Journal of Research in Crime and Delinquency* 24 (1), 49-68.

*In the revision of this chapter, for inclusion in the new book, invaluable assistance was generously given by Darryl Plecas, Tonita Murray and Donald Loree. Most recently Curtis Clarke was most generous in devoting a great deal of his time in thorough reviewing the chapter. The critical contribution of Darryl, Toni, Don and Curtis is most gratefully acknowledged.

Chapter 4

Police Power and Effectiveness

The German Police

"Terrifying are the weaknesses of power." Greek Proverb

Introduction

During his study of the German police through field observation, the observing author acquired the impression and understanding that German police are a strongly designed force for exercising state powers. However, despite this apparently unmistakable symbolism of power and strength associated with them, the police in Germany seem lacking in real power. They seem isolated from the people they are required to serve. Their frustration, despair and lack of ability to make an apparent dent on the ongoing criminal situation have promoted the authors to join several other observers of the German police to state that the police should seek strength in popular support. It is this new philosophy that will help them develop a new sense of real power based on their ability to work with the people as their partners. It is with this premise in mind that the chapter explores how "terrifying are the weaknesses of power" in regard to the German police. It will be argued in the chapter that the German police will overcome this weakness with the new approach suggested here.

Historical political framework and police

In Germany the police are controlled by the governments in the states or the *Länder*. Arntz (1968) observed that in the past there were "communal" police organizations in some states with "the *Land* police play the predominant role," because the gendarmerie was a state authority. Today, he adds, "so far as the police are concerned, the *Länder* are responsible for legislation and its execution." Nevertheless, one will be mistaken in suggesting that direct control by state governments makes the police an "army." The police are controlled nationally in New Zealand or Finland, and the police in Australia or Japan are organized as state police forces (in Japan the states are smaller entities known as prefectures). None of these police forces could be considered an "army." Police observers have maintained that "centralization of police and democracy is possible" (Bookbinder, 1981; Berkeley, 1969). But the state-controlled police system in Germany tends to transmit somewhat different signals.

Fogelson (1977) mentions that, "Americans had a firm belief that the police should be controlled by local officials," because "a state police, like the German Polizei" appear "undesirable." They, Fogelson argues, felt that "a military force ... like the German *Polizei,"* was "a threat to their civil liberties and political right." In his 1915 text, *European Police System,* Fosdick noted that local control of the police is an anathema because of German socio-political culture. He says that "with the exception of Leipzig and Stuttgart, the important cities of Germany are debarred from local control." It is "on the whole unfavorably regarded in Germany." Fosdick notes that the locally controlled police forces like the one in Stuttgart are "demoralized" because of "personal interests and party politics." He adds:

> State supervision is of course effective at the expense of popular control. The System is autocratically centralized. Citizens are given no opportunity to express their opinion of the police. The issue is never raised at the polls, nor under the present system could it be raised. As a matter of fact, in the Anglo-Saxon sense of the term, there is no such thing as democratic administration in Germany; in its place is a huge bureaucratic machine.

The constitution (Edinger, 1986) grants limited powers to the self-governing communities. Although the police powers of the present Ministers of the Interior (Ebsworth, 1960) in the states "were still not as substantial as they had been under the Weimar Republic," (*Weimarer Republik*, [1919-1933]), they have "great powers." One subtle observer (Johnson, 1983) states that the Ministry of the Interior in Germany is one of "the five classic ministries" with "Finance, Justice, Defense and Foreign Affairs," the origins of which could be traced to "nineteenth-century Prussia." However, the "Interior has tended to lose function." Besides the "separation of services" from it, the police are mainly the responsibility of the states. Nevertheless, the Interior still "remains one of the most prestigious and influential of departments." In the "Interior something of the old Prussian rectitude and neutrality vis-à-vis politics survived," and consequently, it operates in a conservative and traditional German administrative way. The Germans "both in and outside of the police, saw localized police as a major obstacle to civil order control" (Fairchild, 1988).

In 1871 when Prince Otto von Bismarck adopted the constitution of the North German Confederation, President Ulysses Grant hailed it as "a desire for speedy progress towards the blessings of democracy" (Craig, 1978). Grant seems to have misinterpreted the intentions of Bismarck who wanted the new constitution to "create the institutions for a national state that would be able to compete effectively with the most powerful of its neighbors." He had no desire to limit "the aristocratic-monarchical order of the pre-national period." The emperor had enormous powers to appoint and dismiss all officials of the federal government and to interpret the constitution. However, among the powers left to the states was their authority and control over the police. Nevertheless, "there was to be no nonsense about popular sovereignty." It was Bismarck's design that the German people were not to enjoy "the dangerous powers that the American people could demand on the basis of their Declaration of Independence and the preamble of the constitution." As Craig explains:

> On the contrary, it was to be clear from the outset that the Reich
> was a gift that had been presented to them and that, if it were not
> properly appreciated, it might be withdrawn. The unspoken
> corollary to Bismarck's constitutional theory . . .was that, if the
> situation warranted it, if the German people did not in fact show

the loyalty and gratitude that their leaders had the right to expect,
then the princes could unmake their own creation and refashion it
in the way they saw fit.

Consequently, German police, controlled by the individual state governments instead of the national government, were to function in a climate of authoritarianism and an undemocratic culture which did not allow a sense of public accountability by the police to become established.

During the Weimar Republic the Central state Police or *Zentrale Staatspolizei* became the first attempt at the centralization of the police. According to Fowler (1979), the Republic's numerically strong and "powerful police" were kept in barracks to handle "the kind of riots, intimidation and violence" which marked those years. However, "this strength was more apparent than real" as the constitution permitted the use of federal police only in the "direst emergency" for a "limited time." Separate states including the city states like Berlin, Bremen and Hamburg controlled the police instead of the central government. In the states that Minister of the Interior was responsible for the day-to-day operation of the police, but the Minister of Justice supervised the investigation and prosecution of crimes. Fowler concludes that the police were not "disloyal" to democracy or "riddled with Nazi sympathizers" when Hitler was "building up his strength." True, the police earned some notoriety when the Berlin Police President in the *Kapp Putsch* in 1920 tried to overthrow the government and replace it with one formed by the extreme right and the attempted coup did show that the police did not develop a sense of accountability to the people.

In the Third Reich, Hermann Goring, the Prussian Minister of the Interior, succeeded in "constructing a political police to enforce the Nazi will by whatever means were necessary" with the Secret State Police or the Gestapo or the *Geheime Staatspolizei,* with the SS or the *Sicherheitsstaffel* and with the SA or the *Sturmabteilung* (Fowler, 1979). Gellately (1990) notes that the Gestapo did not have to be created because "political police existed in most of the federal states before 1933." By 1934 "a separate Prussian police ceased to exist," as they became "subordinated to the Reich." The police became highly centralized under Heinrich Himmler who "commanded the SS Ordinance Troops or the *Verfligungstruppen,* the SD or the *Sicherheitsdienst,* the Gestapo, the SS Death Head battalions or concentration camp guards, the Criminal Police or the German CID, the Order Police, the Border Security Service, the Fire Brigades and the general SS" (Thomaneck, 1985). Police accountability was so disregarded under Himmler that he could order the police to act not on the basis of law but according to "the directives of Hitler, Himmler, and other ministers."

In 1935 a law was enacted (Cook and Paxton, 1986) which "established a novel principle in criminal law that the courts should punish offenses not punishable under the Criminal Code if they were deserving of punishment according to healthy public sentiment." During this period "the police became completely militarized" surpassing the tradition of the Kaiser's days when "the police were used like an army and shot people on the streets" (Ardagh, 1987). The police were asked to "pay particular attention to public morale by ruthlessly dealing with all kinds of potentially defeatist statements in public." They were directed to seek "the full cooperation of the citizenry" in Adolf Hitler's creation of a master race. "In the sphere of racial policies," the Gestapo could depend on the "readiness of the German citizen to provide information on the suspected deviations from the new behavioral norms" (Gellately, 1990). The SS "had since 1934 attracted many university graduate and undergraduate students," and the Gestapo and the SD were infiltrating into student ranks encouraging them to spy on foreign students (Giles, 1985).

After World War II

The allies were determined to ensure "a radical dismantling of this police apparatus at the end of the war" by creating "a democratic police force, or at least a police force that would be appropriate for policing a democratic society"

135

(Fairchild, 1988). She adds that in "abandoning military symbols and emphasizing citizen-friendly operations," German police were able to bring about a new "organizational ethos" as a result of reconstruction after the war. Gemmer (1978) summarizes:

> It actually started in the year 1947-48, but the difference from the previous time is that we now have police on state levels. Our German police during the previous time was a national police on a federal level. But the police–and this is the opinion of all my colleagues–do not feel bad about this, for the police is a bit nearer the scene of crime and criminology. We have well developed cooperation between city, state and federal police in Germany.

The post-war German police strove to attain "a positive image" (Berkeley, 1969) with their slogan, "The Policeman: Your Friend and Helper." The "vigorous" control of "inefficient or abusive police behavior" was accomplished by state legislators through questions directed to the Ministry of the Interior. Berkeley also notes that the German police respected the role of the press in a democracy, and a police recruits' class had "one of the basic books" to remind them of this "reality." He also met reporters who told him that they "rarely encountered a case where the police sought to suppress unfavorable news." Berkeley expresses admiration that "the German police have pressed forward with direct public relations on a variety of fronts," inviting citizens to "inspect" their local police stations, holding police shows, and mounting week-long national police exhibitions. Berkeley found that many police offices serve in "many state legislatures and numerous municipal councils." He notes that there seems to be "fewer in the right-wing" of politics.

It has been observed that no "serious differences" exist between the city administration and the police in Germany, and their cooperation is "nearly always excellent." Individual police officers usually spend their entire careers in a community, because "Germans have strong local ties." The Basic Law has made a provision for localization and regionalization of police administration. According to Article 36, "persons employed in other federal authorities should, as a rule, be drawn from the land in which they serve." The Article also mentions that "the regional ties" of the population in the state shall be reflected in "military laws" (Hucko, 1989).

Following the Allied Occupation, "the British-inspired reorganization" (Ebsworth: 1960) of German police for ensuring local accountability almost completely failed. The British wanted "a balance of powers between Minister of the Interior, police committee and chief of police." However the British police committees to be formed by the *Regierungsbezirk,* an administrative sub-division, could not survive, because the *"Regierungspraesident,* the former police authority" would not accept the arrangement. According to the British plan, the Minster of Interior would have 'general supervisory powers" over the police while the chief of police would be given "full executive control of his force" including internal administration, discipline, and junior promotions. The chief had no "executive superior" and was responsible "only to the law." Liberal-minded Germans felt that in Germany with its "turbulent political past, a militaristic outlook amongst senior officers," a police chief must have a civilian leader as a "perpetual reminder that he and his force were servants of the civilian authority." While the British experiment failed in the old land of Prussia, and an American attempt at decentralization was unsuccessful, the centralized French model was a great success.

An American (Von Koch, 1979) observes that the police are no longer "under central authority" as they were under Hitler and Himmler, but local control is extremely limited. He noted that a "city can only present the problem but the police will offer solution," and they "do not permit any interference with their assignments. Because it is a civil law country, the police in Germany act as an integral part of the administrative apparatus. In Britain where the common law ideology prevails, the police seems independent from the "officials of the magistrate's courts," and their "duties were confined to upholding the criminal law." The identities of the police and the government seem to be continuing

137

closely in Germany. American remedies against "police misconduct" (Hermann, 1981) like exclusionary rules are not considered "efficient" or "necessary" in Germany because the "police are hierarchically organized on the state level." No authority like the Chancellor of Justice in Finland is needed to investigate police misconduct. In the Federal Republic of Germany, the guardians of law and order are considered to be "efficiently controlled through inner-official supervision." According to Feltes (1988) there existed nothing like, "the work of the McDonald Commission of Canada or Police complaints authorities."

Traditionally bureaucratic organizational structure

Although this has very largely changed today, only until a few years back, the police in Germany were organized into an elaborate hierarchy and a long chain-of command. At the lowest level, a police officer is a *Polizeiwachtmeister* after a year while he is still being trained. Following the completion of training after two and a half years, he is promoted to the rank of *Polizeihauptwachtmeister*. He can then become a *Polizeimeister*. After four more years he may be given the rank of *Polizeiobermeister*. Finally, in approximately ten years he attains the rank of a *Polizeihauptmeister* or Sergeant. Any *Polizeihauptwachtmeister* may take the examination for the *Kommissar* Academy training after one year at the *Bereitschafspolizei* or the Task Force Police unit and a year at a *Polizeirevier* or a police station. The ranks of command officers or *Offizier* are *Kommissar* or Captain, *Erster Hauptkommissar* or senior Captain, *Polizeirat* or Major, *Oberrat* or Colonel, *Direktor* or Director, and *Praesident* or Commissioner. Although the police President *is* a civilian, one director in the department, the local *Landespolizeidirektor* may be the higher ranking police executive with regular training. The Leading Directors or the *Leittende Direcktoren* are higher in rank than *Polizei Direktoren*. In the detective branch, command officers are called *Kriminalkommissar, Kriminaloberkommissar, Kriminalhauptkommissar* and *Erster Kriminalhaupkommissar*.

The German police service has three levels of officers: intermediate, supervisory and senior. In the German public bureaucracy, the "inferior" public servants are found in the postal service, the federal railway service, and some other non-police services. In the public service, pay grades are from A1 to B4, but the police pay scales are A5-A10 for intermediates, A9-A13 for supervisors and A13-B4 for seniors. Until recently, an A1 salary range is $7,000 to $8,000 annually: A5 is $8,500 to $10,000, and A9 is $11,000 to $16,500. A13 is $17,000 to $27,000, and B4 is $28,000 to $65,000. This hierarchy of ranks, levels, pay grades, and salaries reflects a tradition of authority and power in German police.

In the post-war years (Fairchild, 1988) "there is also a civil leadership at the local level;" police presidents *are* "political appointees." They are generally jurists" who have served in other civil service positions such as prosecutors or judge, "prominent trade union leaders, and "more unusually a civil servant from a non-legal back ground. "Career police officers may "occasionally" become police chiefs but only as "political appointees." In 1990 when the Social Democratic Party was running the government, the police president in Hamburg was a civil servant in the Education Department before his transfer to the Police Department. The last police President in Hamburg was a Trade Union leader in the *Deutscher Gewerkschaftsbund,* the German Union Federation. In Frankfurt, the police President served in the *Bundeskriminalamt* or the Federal Office of Criminal Investigation before his appointment. Although civilian chiefs are actively involved in policy–making, "the more a civilian chief gets involved in the day-to-day operations of a police agency, the more he is likely to incur the resentment of the career officers" (Fairchild, 1988). Berkeley (1969) comments that civilian police chiefs in Germany, "simply regard police work as normal governmental administration." They do not view it as more "esoteric or special than any other branch of governmental activity." Fosdick (1915) explains that the practice of not having as police chief anyone "who has not had some previous experience in governmental work" enables the large police departments to function as "state institutions constituting an integral part of the great web of officialdom which centers about the state ministries." In any case the practice of civilian chiefs is not a guarantee against the police institutions. The leadership of one person is not enough to alter the entire police organizational culture. Much depends on how the political leadership wants the police to develop.

Heinrich Himmler was a civilian "in his capacity as chief of the German Police as the *Reichsführer* of the SS and received his orders directly from Hitler" (Ziegler, 1989). He fashioned the SS as the most dependable force of his chief's personal dictatorship. A civilian chief may see himself like the typical" German official sees himself as a source of professional policy advice, qualified by experience and training to offer authoritative opinions both on what should be done and how" (Johnson, 1983). He also "appreciates the importance of political masters." With his "long tenure, more specialized knowledge, and greater familiarity with the complexities of the administrative world," the civilian police chief plays an important role in policy-making, although "the authority of the politician is greater." In accordance with the traditional German notions, "bureaucrats and politicians are both holders of public power and agenda of the state." Even today "traditional concepts live on."

Within the *Vollzugspolizei* or the executive police are the *Schutzpolizei* or the uniformed police, or the *Kriminalpolizei* or the plainclothes detectives, and the Task Force Police or the *Bereitschaftspolizei*. The latter are quartered in barracks and kept in reserve as an armed unit to reinforce normal police operations. Located throughout the country, the Task Force Police are equipped with motor vehicles, telecommunications, and weapons by the central government in Bonn. These supplies include (Kasti, 1982) "special vehicles," explosive devices, water cannons with a capacity of 9,000 liters, and the extensive stock of operational equipment to provide "the officers with the best possible protection." These units are used increasingly against "mass demonstrations" and "mass meetings." At the Task Force Police Unit Headquarters, "quick apprehension training," "motorcycle driving, "and "riot-drills" are conducted through prolonged training sessions. In a course on handling demonstrations, the recruits are taught by the *Bereitschaftsoffiziere* or the Task Force Police officers how to identify the leaders of a mass demonstration and how to apprehend them without allowing the rest of the demonstrators to protest against the police actions. The security police who have been called "the peculiar German Institution" (Fairchild, 1990) operate as military personnel, and on orders from their superiors, they use strong-arm tactics. According to Kasti, the use of the Task Force Police personnel has increased in Hessen because of the "replacement individual service with pairs and small groups from the ranks." The Task Force Police are utilized today twelve times more in the state of Hessen than in the 1960s. A young recruit, as a *Polizeihauptwachtmeister,* is attached at least for a year to the Task Force Police for training. According to Helfer and Siebel (Quoted in Fairchild, 1990), "training of 16-year-old recruits should not be combined with civil order control work, since the emphasis on such training is unduly militaristic."

The Federal Border Police or the *Bundesgrenzschutz* (BGS) guard the borders of the country. They have "a varied security role" (Ardagh, 1987). A special law allows the Border Police to be deployed anywhere "in the event of a serious internal emergency in terms of the Basic Law" (Nebelin, 1982). The Basic Law also allows the BGS "to be entrusted with special tasks throughout the federal territory in case of tensions." Amended in 1968 and 1972, Articles 35 provides for the deployment of the BGS:

> In order to maintain or restore public security or order, a *Land* may, in cases of particular importance, call forces and facilities of the Federal Borders Guard to assist its police if, without this assistance the police could not, or only with considerable difficulty, fulfill a task.

On the day, June 24, 1968, when Articles 35 was amended, a new provision was inserted in Article 20 to give citizens the right to resist any person or persons seeking to abolish constitutional order. It seems as if the lawmakers were concerned that the availability of the BGS to maintain order was going to restrain the rights of the people.

The BGS personnel carry "typical police weapons such as side arms," "spray devices of irritants," "pistols, sub-machine guns and batons," and "precision rifles and machine guns as well as explosives and incendiary material." In addition, "a great variety of special cars are at the disposal of these police units such as armored cars, water cannons, etc." The Border Police, like the Task Force Police, "support operational units" of the ordinary police, and "they are also deployed to deal with public emergencies" (Nabelin, 1982). They are very militaristic.

Thomaneck (1985) mentions that the police are overworked today. While "in 1981 overtime amounted to approximately ten million hours," there has also been "an increase in the actual police forces of around thirty percent between 1969 and 1980." Accordingly, the police density of 1:400 in 1969 has reached 1:351. Feltes (1988) argues that "nobody controls the effectiveness of the German police." He adds that financial crises do not seem to affect police expansion. Violent demonstrations, rising crime rates, and terrorism are cited for justifying increasingly higher allocations of resources to the police.

State-mandated police task

In Germany "the duties of the police are restricted to the preservation of law and order" (Arntz, 1968). The police no longer perform administrative functions which are considered to be conducive to public contacts and friendly relations with the public. Many police leaders (Tanner; Haggkvist, 1988) in Finland where these functions are police responsibilities of general service to citizens appreciate the beneficial effects of these tasks. The Germans (Kratz, 1984) emphasize "crime control," "safety," and "order in traffic circulation." They take responsibility for "internal security at mass meetings, catastrophes and riots." They are responsible for "fighting against threatening dangers to ... the liberal democratic basic order." In his capacity as a leader of the Christian Democratic Union and the Christian Social Union opposition, Helmut Kohl advocated stronger powers for the police to maintain order (Thomaneck, 1985). Franz Josef Strauss of the CSU ridiculed the "concept of the police as social referee or social engineer" as a "mere fancy." Strauss insisted that the police should engage themselves in the "ruthless implementation of the law," "the prevention of crime," the "execution of state authority," and the "elimination of the ideas giving rise to terrorism."

Katzenstein (1987) comments that "the traditional strong role of the administrative police" has now disappeared. Although "debate about a new, comprehensive police law" has had no results, he states that "through various piecemeal reforms the police has de facto been given its new, preventive task." The police have acquired "computerized data archives that contain a vast amount of information about individuals...elaborate statistical profiles of probable suspects," and he adds that "coercion" has not "become less necessary in West Germany's semisovereign state." Heiland (1992) maintains that just before the unification of two Germanies, "the social control net" was "spreading." He observes:

> It is obvious that the extent of control does not necessarily have to decline ... Individuals whose cases have been dismissed are being sanctioned. Law violators are not only repulsed by specialized forms of social control, (police, prisons, homes, and clinics) but also by welfare institutions and schools, which are becoming more and more sources of control.

Hermann (1981) states that "petty misdemeanors" now related as "petty infractions" have been removed from the criminal process. Since sanctions against infractions are within the competence of administrative authorities, the police play a "primary role" in imposing fines for "violations of traffic laws as well as of business and trade regulations." Accordingly, in "police operations at demonstrations"(Ruckriegel, 1986) in North Rhine - Westphalia, use is made of police authority to handle "administrative offenses" which enables them to "punish" demonstrators if public safety and peace is "impaired" or "disturbed." The police made extensive use of their powers in traffic offenses. In countries like Finland, the fines imposed by the police are approved by judges, but in the Federal Republic "the judiciary gets involved only if an accused files a complaint." After criticism that some German companies were helping Libya build a chemical weapon plant, *The Wall Street Journal* (January 26,1989) reported that as the "Bonn government continued to come under political criticism," there was "an escalation of official efforts to uncover West German links to the Libya project." It would seem that the police were confiscating files in accordance with the priorities set by the government.

In the Federal Republic of Germany, the police "carry out investigations" (Hermann, 1981), because preliminary investigation by "an investigating magistrate was abolished in 1975 as it tended to duplicate investigations already done by the police." As Hermann remarks, "warrants are not used" for house searches "since police and the prosecutors usually manage to induce citizens to consent" to searches. In *The Wall Street Journal* report of German and Libyan connections, it was mentioned that when the "prosecutors had acquired decisive leads," officials "showed up at their doors," "raided the offices of companies and homes of individuals suspected of helping Libya," and "confiscated personal correspondence and office files from Imhausen, two other companies and 12 homes." The police were not barred by many constraints. Fowler (1979) states that "German criminal law is based on the inquisitorial principle," and the "object" of the trial is the "pursuit of truth in which both prosecutor and defense counsel cooperate." However, for the public prosecutor, every criminal case must end in "conviction," and defense lawyers are totally unscrupulous in exploiting every weakness in a case to triumph over the prosecutor. Fowler adds that "according to some German policemen," on occasion "lawyers have actually joined terrorist groups ... or cooperated with them in acting as links between detained terrorists and accomplices outside."

Incapacities of the police against crime including drugs

In spite of their marked identity with the state, their strong organizational hierarchy, and their conspicuous social control role, the police complain of powerlessness. They perceive that society, politicians, courts, and academics are unsympathetic. During the field study by the observer author, in Frankfurt the local police were engaged in an anti-drug experiment called "Argos." They sought to induce drug dealers and users to move to more observable locations to prevent the increasing expansion of drug trading. The police were not, however, optimistic about achieving success, because they seemed convinced that they were alone and powerless in the battle against drugs, prostitution, and violence. Those who were engaged in "Argos" felt that the laws concerning drugs and prostitution were very liberal, because liberalism was a political ploy. If the police knew that a prostitute was suffering from Aids, they had no way to stop her from practicing her trade. According to the police, many local politicians, particularly those belonging to the Green Party, were interested in presenting a liberal image. As a result, lax legal provisions dealt with prostitutes, drug-dealers, demonstrators and others. Thomaneck (1985) refers to "the police as the whipping boys of the nation" and to their "frustration and aggression," because the press has written about "neofascist tendencies in the police force," "gruesome police misconduct," and other allegedly reactionary trends.

At the time of the research by the observer author, the police maintained that crime was rising in Frankfurt, a city of about 600,000, compared to Hamburg with a population of *1.5* million. In Frankfurt there were 19,000 crimes for every 100,000 citizens; Hamburg had only 14,000 crimes for every 100,000 people. Police observations are supported by statistics. Felters (1988) states that between 1981 and 1987 Frankfurt had almost a 50 percent increase in crime as against 22, 34, 14 and 6 percent in Hamburg, Hanover, Berlin and Munich, respectively. In

1988 certain offenses in the whole country had registered sharp increases. Included among them were violent offenses like "robbery, extortion by means of threats and highway robbery in motor vehicles" (2.8 percent), "slight bodily injury with intent" (7.78 percent), "insult, assault and battery" (8.1percent), and "drug offenses" (13.3 percent). Total crime, however, decreased in 1988 (4,356,726 crimes in a population of 61,241,700) compared to 1987 (4,444,108 crimes in a population of 61,140,500) as reported by the Federal Criminal Police Office Bundeskriminalamt, 1988). Although "the criminal statistics of the police" are not a true reflection of "the actual situation as far as crime is concerned," they are "close to reality" and are "an aid for legislative and executive powers." Sessar (1991) mentions the unreliability in crime statistics because "the police sometimes use rather crude, idiosyncratic, re-simplification rules based on their own experience." According to Gemmer (1978), the "unreported crime rate in Germany is about ten times as high as crime figures registered by the police." Brusten (1987) bluntly states that the police seem to manipulate crime statistics "for their own purposes: such as claims for more manpower, increase in financial resources and better equipment."

Feltes (1988) notes a reduction of 25 percent in the number of calls to the police in spite of the increase in crime in Frankfurt. Although Feltes does not correlate the decreasing calls with the deteriorating social image of the police, such a correlation may not be wrong. Feltes also cites statistics indication that all calls to the police by city dwellers in Germany are lower than those in Montreal, New York, Toronto, and Chelsea, England.

Lack of rapport with minorities, prostitutes, and soldiers

German police described many groups of resident aliens who were found incapable of conforming to what was considered culturally appropriate standards of behavior. The Frankfurt police were right in their perceptions about the participation of minorities in crime and disorder. Kube (1982) stated that "every fourth suspect encountered in drug trafficking is a foreigner." A large number of drug dealers in Frankfurt were non-German. Koetzsche (1987) claims that "cheap rents" have attracted "foreign tenants" who are mostly Turks to the inner city areas of Hamburg. Although "crime among young Turks rises almost inexorably," the local police are "helpless" because of the "language barrier" and a "lack of understanding of ...culture and of the Islamic religion." As Edinger (1986) states, the problem of "guest workers," which appeared to be "an economically beneficial arrangement," has resulted in "less desirable social consequences." Foreign workers are today "largely social outcasts," considered to be "more prone to commit crimes than Germans," and they "do not enjoy the same political rights" as the nationals. The problems of the police are compounded by the charges of "racial discrimination" (Koetzsche, 1987) against them.

The police complained about other groups. In Frankfurt they expressed serious concerns about the 2,500 registered prostitutes who were an encouragement to criminal behavior including drug trafficking. According to them, many others operated without registration. Many of the 350 homosexual prostitutes committed crimes like robbery, homicide, and assaults against their clients. Police records identified 3,000 drug users and another 2,000 suspects. Most of the 25,000 thefts from cars were related to drug addiction. According to the police, the potential for crime was further increased by 30,000 American soldiers, 250,000 daily commuters to the center of the city, visitors to the permanent exhibition at Expo, and 20 million passengers passing through the airport. Some Frankfurt-based American military officers treated German police officers with a great deal of so-called deference and civility. Police patrol cars had an easy access through the American army area even at night, and American soldiers were quite careful to avoid troubles with German police. One evening while the observer author was on patrol the police responded to a call from a prostitute who complained that two American soldiers had left her without paying for her sexual services. In their search for the men, the police vigorously stopped many cars with occupants resembling the suspects described by the prostitute. A few American soldiers and their friends felt that the police in Germany were considered "tough." They thought that the police would not hesitate to stop and shoot if the driver of an American army transport did not comply with police wishes.

The courts, the prosecutors, the legislators and other public agencies were not, the police complained, reinforcing the laws against drugs, prostitution, and other activities that generated crime. Commenting about the joint efforts of the police and "youth and health authorities" in combating drugs, Kube (1982) mentions that "there are conflicts and antipathies." At one busy location, the police ignored a drug addict who has injected himself and had empty vials lying around him. In a patrol car, the police received a call from a manager of a restaurant who said a customer had locked himself in a restroom. Upon arriving, the police found a person doing drugs inside a rest room but said to the observer author that they were reluctant to bring charges against drug users, because stringent proofs were reportedly demanded in courts. Possession of drugs, the police complained, was difficult to prove, because contraband was secretly delivered at predetermined locations. Most police undercover agents were known to drug traffickers who would hide when the police appeared. The sense of helplessness of the German police contrasted with the Finnish police who felt that their courts were cooperative. Judges in Finland told the observer author that the courts were satisfied with the quality of police investigation and their professional reputation. Perhaps the German courts lack confidence in police fairness and integrity.

German criminal agencies like the Federal Criminal Bureau of *Bundeskriminalamt* have stressed that in the fight against drugs the police would need the co-operation of "the mass media," "the public in general," and "social service agencies" (Kube, 1982). Possibly, that is true. Kube argues that "the current emphasis on police suppressive work alone cannot solve the drug problem." However, in personal interviews (Feltes, 1988; Brusten, 1987), it was learned the police were somewhat shy in seeking the help of others. Such a tradition simply did not exist in Germany; the police did not expect citizens to volunteer to help them. In Frankfurt the special drug project personnel did not mention securing public support for the plan.

Unlike Amsterdam where drug activities seemed concentrated in and around the *Warmoesstraat* district, the famous sailors' quarters, "heroin prostitution," involving women who exchanged sex for heroin, has moved to inner city neighborhoods in Frankfurt. Young women waited at street corners until the early hours of the morning. Visitors to Expo in Frankfurt and other tourists picked these women up for sex and took them to a large, dark parking lot in the downtown area. The police were unable to do anything to halt the behavior and activity, unless an indecent act was performed in public. Younger officers jokingly referred to these sexual acts as "humming" or "making the number." They seemed to be cynically laughing at a world they could not control because of the alleged apathy of all concerned.

While checking prostitutes' licenses in a brothel of inferior status, the police found a few young African women who were registered as prostitutes. They had foreign passports but were able to work as prostitutes because they had documents showing that they were married to Germans. The police knew the marriages were fake, but they did not take any action, because, they said, the Green Party and the Immigration Authorities were "very liberal" about admitting foreigners to the country. They added that almost anyone could enter Germany under the pretext of being a political refugee. The recent fury against foreigners, particularly, refugees would almost certainly test the powers of the police.

The police complained that their strength was inadequate to handle the problems of drugs, prostitution, rising crime, and demonstrations. In Hessen 16,000 police personnel served a population of 2,664,700; consequently, the police density per 1,000 citizens was 1:167, which was high, because the density for the whole country was 1:351 (Thomaneck, 1985), in spite of "an extraordinary increase in manpower and finance." Feltes (1988) reports a reluctance by the authorities to reveal the strength of the police. Becker (1973) reported that approximately 120,000 police personnel were in the Federal Republic in the early 1970s. According to Feltes, the strength today was 170,000 which, compared to the 1970s, showed an increase of approximately 40 percent. Katzenstein (1987) maintained that "the total personnel of all police forces increased from 165,000 in 1965 to 217,000 in 1978." Gemmer (1988) reported that "altogether we have about 250,000 police officers in West Germany." In another article (1978), Gemmer estimated that 156,000 police personnel worked for the states, and 25,000 were federal police officers including 23,000 border guards.

The police also felt that not enough resources were allocated for research to improve police methods and strategies. A top police leader said that a research proposal on the subject of the changes needed for the police in the next century was submitted to the federal government by a high-ranking police-training institute. It was not funded. The politicians, the police complained, were not comfortable with research that might expose their weaknesses.

The politics of protest

In Frankfurt the police considered demonstrations to be a serious problem. In police videotapes of demonstrations, the aggressiveness of the demonstrators was highlighted. The police seemed visibly frustrated by increasing demonstrations. Demonstrations had increased from 1,300 in 1970 to 7,453 in 1984. According to Ruckriegel (1986), the number had "nearly sextupled."

Strong-arm measures dominated police responses to demonstrations and seemed to increase police frustrations. According to Kratz (1986), innovations for handling public protests were not abundant. Generally the police took into account the political situation and the nature of the protests. The police chief's most important concerns in mass disturbances were the ability and willingness of the rank-and-file to adhere to accepted policy. Consequently, the commanders of the personnel engaged in policing demonstrations paid a great deal of attention to communication of orders. It appeared that the sociology of protesting groups, respect for the rights of demonstrators, and other human rights issues did not demand special attention from police policymakers. These views of policymakers are shared by other observers of the German police (Fairchild, 1990; Fowler, 1979; Thomaneck, 1985).

The police were criticized that "the methods and equipment employed in police operations" (Thomaneck, 1985) against demonstrations were militaristic. They were accused of acting as "an instrument for the reduction of (legitimate and constitutional) political conflict to problems of law and order." They were blamed for applying "paramilitary solutions" to "conflicts which cry out for political solutions." They were found unaware that demonstrations, protests and riots were "the symptoms of a steady crisis of West German democracy." The Green Party, whom the police viewed as anarchists, made "attempts to realize democracy beyond the well-defined lobby and party democracy establishment," and the party's new cult of liberty "had resulted directly in a police crisis." According to Fairchild (1984), a unique priority for German police today was control of civil unrest through the use of sophisticated non-lethal weapons. They are developing "specifics of training for leadership in handling police troops." Criticized for their militaristic methods, they demonstrated "a gradual hardening of attitude towards the public." They were frustrated at being "the targets of the public unrest although they are fulfilling their duty to provide order."

The erosion of legitimacy

As can be perceived from the remarks made above, despite their strong statutory powers, paramilitary support elements, and sophisticated technological paraphernalia, German police showed signs of frustration and powerlessness. They felt that their impact on crime, drugs, and disorders was feeble. Their morale resembled that of the police in less affluent nations like India, Thailand and Mexico where salaries were low, resources were limited and their tasks exceeded their capacity.

The status of German police appeared different than that of New Zealand police whose public standing and prestige are very high. For example, the Wellington police knew street kids who were suspected of having AIDS. The police had received confidential private information from doctors and hospitals, because doctors were concerned about police safety and welfare. According to Palmer (1986), "the police are clearly an important political influence in the New Zealand community," and "they enjoy respect." New Zealand politicians ask "for more and more community support for the police," and as a result of public confidence, the police get cooperation from other public agencies. New Zealand was largely free from terrorism and drug-related criminality that characterized Germany and had a homogeneous population except for the Maoris. Such factors helped to reduce suspicion and tension in the environment in which police operated, and certainly the history of New Zealand was not marked by the upheavals that shaped Germany's history.

Camaraderie among public agencies was also high in Finland. Some judges and prosecutors remarked that the police enjoyed a good reputation for fairness and integrity, and consequently, there was no reason not to accept the police versions of criminal cases. Even a large number of prisoners in Finland and New Zealand did not have serious complaints against the police. Prison officials and the police in Finland cooperated with each other, and prison escapees were vigorously pursued and rearrested by the police without acrimony. Like New Zealand, Finland was also a country without the problems of heterogeneity, violent crime and drug-related criminality. Although its history is marked by turbulence including foreign domination under the USSR, it is not as volatile as Germany.

Compared to the police in Finland and New Zealand, German police lacked public confidence and support. Their legitimacy seemed to be increasingly questioned by the post-war generation. Military orientation, rigid obedience, and stern discipline were regarded as valuable qualities for German civil servants including the police. History (Edinger, 1986) taught Germans that for the resolution of domestic and foreign conflicts "a powerful state, strong exclusive leadership, weak legislatures, and minimal participation in policymaking" were necessary. However, (Katzenstein, 1987) the "values have changed," an erosion of the paternalistic bureaucracy had occurred. The "younger voters" supported "new non-material and quality-of-life issues" more enthusiastically than older people. In the 1970's "civil liberties were more secure" than previously, and in the 1980s Green Party members "have attracted a sufficient number of the voting public to have an important effect," although Germany still remained a *Rechtsstaat.*

Training: emphasis on rigor, length, and technicalities

Police training for uniform officers in Germany seemed to be highly structured and very long while the observer author was conducting his field study. According to a senior commander at the National Police Staff College (Kratz, 1984), the police were "thoroughly" trained for their special function, and training is given to three different classes of police officers belonging to the "inferior, intermediate and senior service." "The inferior service" officers were attached to the Police Task Force units that handled serious law and order situations and were "available as a reserve in the case of need." The intermediate service officers were trained at the *Fachhochschule* or professional high schools in the states. The officers of the senior service of the states and the national government received their training "at the *Polizeiführungsakademie,*" the National Police Staff College. As Steven (1983) comments, German Police training was "much more structured than the American approach" and provided "specific training programs ... for each level within the police rank structure."

Inferior service recruits went to one of the thirty state police schools for two-and-one-half years. According to Kratz (1986) of the National Police Staff Colleges, these recruits either completed high school or *Gymnasium (65* percent), or came from an intermediate school or Realschule *(35* percent). Education in a *Gymnasium* prepared a student for a university, and "this type of school is intended to provide a general education of high standard" (Arntz, 1968). The intermediate school prepared students for medium-grade posts in offices or advanced professional schools called *Fachschulen.* Consequently, the inferior service recruits came to the job with a purely basic education. Their future training was expected to provide them with a professional education for further advancement in the service.

In the first year cadets received theoretical training in laws including the penal code, criminal procedure, and other acts and statutes. They were taught social sciences like psychology, sociology, and ethics. They were trained in weapons, physical skills, sports, and self-defense. During the next year, they were taught criminal investigation, first aid, typewriting, car driving, boat driving, radio communications, and some law. They were sparingly used in crowd control, generally as reserve units.

Training was lengthy, programs were structured, trainees were regularly paid, and they lived a cloistered existence in the academies. Recruits worked with a formation of the Task Force Police for tough emergency task. They were only sixteen years of age when they entered the police and remained until the age of sixty; Steven (1983) comments that "most officers are facing roughly forty years of service," which offered "a full range of educational and training programs" for those demonstrating "the basic capabilities of rising to the highest rank." Salaries were "satisfactory." The chief of the Task Force Police in Schleswig-Holstein had a salary equivalent to that of a university professor (Thomaneck, *1985).* Steven adds that most police officers "have no interest in leaving the salary since they usually know very little about other occupations." Consequently, "turn over" rates were low.

At the police school in Hamburg, *Landespolizeischule,* (Reise, Londorf and Klonz, 1990) they had sixteen teachers, thirteen of whom were *Pokizeihauptkommissar* or high ranking police personnel and three were civilian teachers for English, German, mathematics, biology, and politics. A police candidates went there as a *Polizeiwachtmeister,* the lowest entry level rank, for two and half years. After one year of study, the recruits were sent for six months of practical training. Before they went on to practical training, they had to pass an examination which entitled them to the rank of *Polizeioberwachtmeister.* Following the completion of practical training, the recruits returned to the police school for one more year, passed another examination, and would then be promoted to the rank of *Polizeihauptwachtmeister.* They had to be attached to the Task Force Police at least for one year. After one year with the Task Force Police and another year at the police station or *Polizeirevier,* the police officers in Hamburg could take an examination to enter the higher ranking *Kommissar* (police captains or above) training academy. For three years intermediate service officers entered one of fifteen *Fachhochschulen* or colleges of public administration with specialization in police science. Training fell into six periods of six months each. Among the subjects taught to the officers were law psychology, sociology, management, operational tactics, criminology, and criminalistics.

According to Kratz (1984) of the National Police Staff College or the *Polizezfuhrungsakademie,* "in the two years of training" this school sought to ensure that the "candidates for the senior police service" learned to "lead larger police departments and police units," "manage police operations in command and control centers," "fulfill special tasks," and "participate in training and advanced training of police officers." Besides training of senior police commanders, this academy provided refresher courses. During the first year when officers are in their own states they were required to familiarize themselves with state laws, prosecutors' offices, judges, the press and other agencies. In the second year they learned theories of leadership, principles of management, operational tactics, social sciences, criminalistics, law, and criminology. Psychology was included in the curriculum "for the longest period" among the social sciences, which included ethics, pedagogy, police science, and sociology. During the second year, officers live in the academy.

To reach a command position, a police officer may need two-and-one-half years of inferior service training, three years training in an intermediate school, and two years of training in an intermediate school, and two years at the senior service academy. Police training in Europe was elaborate and specific for patrol officers, junior commanders, and senior commanders. In England, training programs existed for constables besides the junior and senior command courses at the Bramshill Police College, and training in India, Thailand, Japan, Australia, and New Zealand were extensive. Nowhere was training as elaborate and lengthy as it is in Germany.

German Police training had some attractive features like thoroughness, a life-long career affiliation, and projection of police work as a serious profession. However, the training assumed historical and traditional notions. One of them was the militarism of the police. Historically, "the police of the Empire" (Fairchild, 1984), were found to be "imitative of the military ... and jealous of their greater prestige." Germans had learned to "look to the state for authoritative guidance and expected its leaders to ensure order and harmony." Many "civil servants" welcomed the Nazi regime and Hitler because of the "elimination of parliamentary controls and the concentration of executive power in one hand." Traditionally, "political order and stability" (Edinger, 1986) in Imperial Germany was controlled through "paternalistic public authority" and "the executive and administrative officials" served the interests of the state rather than the people." In post-war Germany the ideal of "a new *Rechtsstaat,* a state governed under law rather than by capricious rulers," embraced the notion that "public authorities are responsible for the collective welfare of the present and the future citizens of the Federal Republic." However, for most Germans the state was not "an expression of the will of the people but...an abstract organizational entity." Today young Germans "feel particularly free to criticize public officials and policies," but state officials were "expected to adhere to the rules of the constitutional order." Deeply held national beliefs like impersonal public authority, identity of government officials with the "state," and militarism continued to define the philosophy of police training. The prolonged exposure to programs marked by these beliefs produced police officers who tended to believe they are professional elitists.

Police selection standards seemed to reinforce their unique mentality. According to Kratz (1986), the National Police Staff College recently invited all senior commanders to construct a profile of the police officer to establish nationwide recruitment guidelines. The number of recruits was fairly large. Steven (1983) mentioned that in North-Rhine-Westphalia, there were 10,000 applicants for 2,200 positions. Gemmer (1978) thought the police were "fortunate" in the recruitment and selection of applicants, "for instance if there is need for about 20 police officers we would have about 500 applicants."

The selection and training of the Metropolitan Police in the United Kingdom particularly during its formative years revealed some glaring contrasts with the German Police. Sir Robert Peel's police were presented to the British public as citizens in uniform. They came from Britain's countryside outside of London. They were honest, hardy and morally strong men. Their wages were low, which helped to maintain their status as ordinary citizens. Their training consisted of simple precepts of behavior and crime prevention. They were regarded not as guardians or watchdogs but as partners of the common man. Although the attrition rates of the German police were very low, they were very high during the early years of the Metropolitan Police, because many men were found unfit to live up to the simple, homespun and human percepts of everyday policing.

Prisoners of tradition and history

The German police enjoyed conspicuous powers given to them in statutes. Their physical capacity could be considered strongly based on their possession of weapons and personnel in special forces. Nevertheless, they seemed powerless in mobilizing support to accomplish their basic tasks.

The hospitality, warmth, and friendly nature of the German police officers were attractive; they welcomed guests with a choice of wine even at police stations. How could such cynical opinions about the public and non-police agencies coexist with the geniality and good sense that police officers so readily displayed? Was there a dichotomy between their official and informal selves? Some German police officers seemed to have accepted their occupation as a job to be done. They learned to live with its frustrations, while they did not seem to be uncomfortable with their powers which they exercised routinely. A large number of officers had exciting hobbies. A junior commander in Frankfurt was a feature writer of police stories for which he traveled around the world. Another command officer was an avid student of Indian culture and was making plans to take a group of interested tourists to India. Another officer of the inferior service was interested in traveling and interior designing. Such varied and interesting hobbies must have been great diversions from these officers' jobs. Many German officers like their counterparts in other affluent countries such as Italy, New Zealand, and Australia were not overtly promotion-minded. They were happy with what their jobs offered: security, material benefits, action, and variety. They were not responsible for the demonstrations, violence, crime, and drugs that were challenging them. The police regretted that they lacked support of the public and public agencies in their efforts against these challenges. They suggested that public acceptability would likely help them be more effective in policing protests, drugs, and crime.

After prolonged research Jager (1984) of the *Polizeführungsakademie* felt that "more emphasis on the psychological aspects" and "verbal skills" were needed to avoid the young Germans' "potential for aggression - often aggravated by previous negative contacts with the police." He suggests that "public education," "informing the public about the police powers," and stressing how the public was "obligated to cooperate with the police" would help. Ruckriegel (1986) of the Ministry of the Interior in North Rhine-Westphalia claimed that German police could escape bitterness and blame in the handling of mass protest if they "maintain a neutral attitude toward legitimate subjects of protest," developed a "willingness ... to talk to organizers," and took steps to "make sure that the demonstration takes a peaceful course," and accept "psychological guidance." Kube (1982) of the *Bundeskriminalamt* advocated "closer cooperation between police and the public," and added that "a return to good old-fashioned policing methods" was called for like "foot patrols" and "crime prevention by education."

Thomaneck (1985) suggests that the police should not regard "the gun" as the symbol of reassurance. Because the death penalty is "unconstitutional" in Germany, the police need to be sensitive to the fact that everywhere in the Federal Republic, they are permitted to fire a "shot aimed to kill." Thomaneck observes that the police themselves are suffering from "dissatisfaction" from "an "inordinate amount of paperwork," "overtime demands," "having to establish authority all the time," and "monotonous routine." They would like to be involved in "community policing" which is demanded of them by those who say there "seems to be a growing gap between the police and the public." Fairchild (1984), deplores that the police leadership continues to favor a "cohesive and disciplined...military style of organization." The public, however, seems to be asking the police to work with them, and perhaps they can work together.

Feltes (1988) claimed that because "violent demonstrations," "terrorism," and the "use of force" caused "great frustrations among German police officers and discontentment with their profession," some "younger officers" wanted to get involved in helping functions. Because "citizens call the police to solve very

159

different problems," he suggested that "the role and the function of the German police has to be discussed again with some new considerations." Brusten (1987) suggested that the police should not be interested "in using criminal statistics for their own purposes: such as claim for more manpower, increase in financial resources and better equipment." He suggested openness and a change of attitude by the police to act in partnership with the people.

Many historical and social factors account for the unique situation of German police, and the reunification of Germany in 1991 has not changed these factors. In spite of tremendous upheavals and national progress, the "earlier philosophy of a *Polizeistaat* ... a paternalistic but intrusive public order in which the state was supposed to rule for the good of the people" (Fairchild, 1988) continues to have its impact in a reunited Germany. People continue to view the police as more of "an organ of the state than the symbol of community power." Craig (1978) claims that "inherited attitudes" and "traditional mental patterns" have not changed, and even today democratic values did not alter the attitude of "deference to authority that was a fixed characteristic of German political attitudes in the eighteenth and nineteenth century." He finds that the "three-point credo" of Germans is: "the state equals the officials; politics destroys character, and the best government is a good administration." These beliefs are not conductive to people-oriented policing. Beyme (1983) also refers to the "authoritarian structure in German families, the apathetic political culture, and the legalistic bias of the majority." Added to these sociological characteristics is the fact that "Germany traditionally had a higher proportion of civil servants than the Anglo-Saxon countries." In the civil service, "the monopoly of lawyers is still unbroken," signifying an abstract legal basis of administration. He explains that with lawyers' connections with "the upper strata of society", the civil servants "score higher on the scale of state-orientation and loyalty."

Bark and Gress (1989) argue that German "society was still psychologically crippled by Nazism." Germans cannot "overcome the past," because they still retain "a deep-rooted inability to meet the world (more) on a human level than on the level of power and force." Dahrendorf (1967) argues that the old world German

> elites have experienced the gradual and parallel destruction of their established social type and their uniform political attitude ... The destructive process has not, however, led to the construction of a political class that gives expression to the competing diversity of social forces and is capable of supporting a liberal democracy.

There are also "the un-political Germans" for whom "politics never became a national passion or a respected part of national culture." They "express the notion of a nonpolitical and impartial bureaucracy implementing parliamentary legislation" (Katzenstein, 1987).

In a reunited Germany

On October 3, 1990, East Germany ceased to exist as a nation. With the destruction of the Berlin Wall in 1989 the West Berlin police found it difficult to adjust to the crime rate increase; the East German police found it impossible to deal with. The East German police lacked the training and equipment to deal with violent situations. In addition, the East German police lacked discretion in making decisions. As a result of the Berlin Wall coming down the East German government had lost its legitimacy; and the police as the arm of the government had lost its authority. Following the Berlin Wall's destruction in November 1989 until elections in 1990 a vacuum existed until East Germany became integrated into West Germany, making a unified German country (Cooper, 1996: 244).

Shortly after the fall of the Berlin Wall cooperation between the East and West German police began. In Berlin, the police chiefs of the east and west were connected by direct telephone. It was not unusual for the East German police to seek the advice of their West German counterparts in dealing with various types of crimes. The West German police even held seminars for their East German counterparts in West Germany. Informally, the police cooperated in solving crimes that involved crossing borders. The rank and file of the East German police, in early 1990, made demands for better working conditions, better pay, and civil service status (Cooper, 1996: 245-246).

Following unification, West German structures and laws were imposed onto East Germany. An example of this is the complete absorption of the East Berlin police by the West Berlin police force. In East Germany, similar to West Germany the control of the police was decentralized and given to the control of the states. Upon unification, East German police officers had to apply into acceptance into the police force. They were required to complete a long detailed questionnaire about their political and professional background before acceptance to the police force. The former East German police officers training was not recognized and higher-ranking officers had to take a demotion in rank. Older, senior police officers were rarely retained. With unification, East German officers had to be trained in the West German system. Many West German police forces established partnerships with East German cities and regions and provided training for local East German police forces. The German unification seemed ideal with East Germany, including the police, adopting the structures, concepts, and institutions of West Germany (Cooper, 1996, p. 248-250).

Need for popular support

Community policing in Germany is limited in contrast to American attempts to innovate community policing into their police forces. Although police departments in Canada, Great Britain and the United States have problems with misunderstanding and trust by community people Germany has a more serious difficulty. These difficulties as explained above are based on historical and legal factors. The police continue to lack "lack of public support, legal restrictions on the exchange of information between different agencies, lack of officer discretion, and structural constraints" (Gramckow, 1995: 17-18). Further, either by the individual German states and federal law, the mission, duty, organization, practices, and procedures of local police departments are determined. The fact that local police in Germany are a subdivision of the state police works to limit community-policing efforts. The individual local police community districts are at a geographical distance from the central police authority and this is also a factor in discouraging community policing. Generally, local police departments have limited authority to empower their supervisors and line officers or to eliminate any segments of their hierarchy, which would allow them to respond to community policing strategies. Another major factor that interferes with the community policing philosophy is the checks and balances created by the division between the Department of Interior and the Department of Justice at the state and Federal levels. The centralized police structure does not allow local police chiefs to have much influence on individual police officer assignments or even with the composition of their police force. The state level determines the assignment of police officers and the number of officers assigned to a local police chief (Gramckow, 1995: 25-26).

However, police effectiveness can come from popular support and enthusiasm, German police might experiment with a few tentative, incremental and simple changes. More police agencies should begin to practice community policing as is in vogue in Hamburg. Interested members of the public and researchers might be encouraged to help adopt a more open policy in the police establishments. Since the police are like "a kind of secret and hidden institution" (Feltes, 1988), these "life-long civil servants" do not customarily feel accountable to the public "to justify their work."

Part of the extensive training at various levels might be replaced by general education at the universities. At the entry level, the police might seek candidates with higher education, if they can be attracted to apply for police positions. Police officers might be encouraged to further their education through incentives. Instructors at the police academies are now police officers at the inferior officer level. At the *Fachhochshule* and the *Polizezführungsakademie* there are also civilian academics as instructors. However, at the lower level, civilian instructors are also needed. Unfortunately, the police leadership has been unwilling to disengage the Task Force Police from training recruits. Gradually removing them from instructing cadets was suggested by a team of sociologists from the University of Saarbrücken (Fairchild, 1987).

German police should be inspired, because Germans are capable of an "enormously disciplined effort" (Schmidt, 1989) as the post-war recovery and reconstruction proved. In the 1960s, young Germans men and women were openly and vehemently protesting publicly, but they displayed discipline and social concern. German bureaucracy has been a great source of reform, and the police can draw inspiration from it. As Schmidt adds, "the reform-minded bureaucrats who were leaders of most states during the period of 1806 and 1820 viewed popular participation in public affairs as a valuable alley. Germans have matchless thoroughness in training (Gaugler, 1990). Organizations encourage employee growth, mobilizing "institutional participation...in the management of the firm" (Weaver, 1990). In making suggestions for police reform in America, the National Advisory Commission on Criminal Justice Standards and Goals (1973) has praised the "rare commitment" in Germany to police training. History and world admiration should be a source of inspiration for the police to try innovation in the newly united Germany.

The German police have their functions spelled out in legal details and the means of performing these functions are often expressed in general and vague terms. It appears the police in Germany find themselves in situations not knowing how to deal with potential criminal violators. For example, in demonstrations the police are required to negotiate with demonstrators and establish a police-free demonstrations zone. The German police appear to be more reactive than proactive with 90 percent of recorded crimes coming from citizens with approximately 5 percent discovered by the police (Kube, 1997: p. 101-102).

Progress has been made by the German police in crime prevention at the local community level through approaches that are targeted at multiple-offenses and focused on violent crimes. The police Germany may reflect on these issues (Kube, 1997: p. 105-113):

1. The actual contribution of the police to the maintenance of internal security appears to vary by region and type of crime. It cannot yet be determined, however, to what extent greater intensity of intervention in criminal law enforcement is more likely to produce greater success in the long term than a more permissive approach

2. The "Second Code", in the sense of rules for the application of law, may well overshadow written criminal and police law significantly with respect to some offense categories. To the extent that this is true, the police contribute to internal security in a manner not directly prescribed by law.

3. Prevention is clearly neglected in police work. With the exception of the national Criminal Police Prevention Program, a mass-media public-information project, it is left for the most part to local initiatives. In the area of drug-related crime in particular, concepts in which prevention is treated as an inter-agency responsibility shared by society at large are solely lacking.

4. As a constantly present institution, the police—as is evident in cases involving domestic disputes—are often called upon even when, in terms of their assigned functions and training, they are not in fact the most appropriate institution under the circumstances. Thus the ability of the police to contribute to conflict resolution and thus to the maintenance of internal security is often questionable, particularly with respect to minor criminal offences.

5. Potential opportunities for prevention in the fight against organized crime could be exploited and developed in a much more systematic

way. In this context, a logistical concept would provide a particularly effective basis for police and inter-agency prevention program.

6. The fight against organized crime is characterized in particular by the conflict that exists between the requirements of law enforcement and those of protection against potential dangers.

7. Crime is one of the potential consequences of technological progress. This fact should be taken into consideration in assessing the possible consequences of technological change.

8. The police will be able to fulfill their responsibilities with respect to crime control only if they exploit to up-to-date technology to the extent possible in support of the future sophistication of criminalistics, and especially forensic investigative methods.

9. The police play only a very limited role in shaping the sense of security/the degree of fear of crime with a population. Fear of crime is an aspect of crime prevention.

Similar to other police agencies throughout the world the German police are the focus of attention and expected to maintain order in society. However, what is often missed is that in a democratic country the police are limited in what they can do to prevent crime.

References

Ardagh, John. 1987. *Germany and the Germans*. London: Hamish Hamilton.

Arntz, Helmut. 1968. *Facts about Germany*. Bonn: The Press and Information Office.

Babbie, Earl. 1986. *The Practice of Social Research*. Belmont, CA: Wadsworth. Bark, Dennis L. and Dacid R. Gress. 1989. *Democracy and Its Discontents*, 1963 - 1988. Cambridge, MA.: Basil Blackwell, Inc.

Becker, Harold K. 1973. *Police Systems of Europe: A Survey of Selected Police Organizations*. Springfield, IL.: Charles C. Thomas.

Berkeley, George E. 1969. *The Democratic Policeman*. Boston, MA: Beacon Press.

Beyme, Klaus Von, 1983. *The Political System of the Federal Republic of Germany*. Hunts, England: Gower Publishing Company Ltd.

Bookbinder, Paul, 1981. The Weimer Police Experiment. *Police Studies* 4 (2), 28-43.

Brunsten, Manfred. 1986. Crime Trends in West Germny: The Use and Usefulness of CrimeStatistics for Criminal Policy. In M. Brusten, J. Graham, N. Herrger, and P. Malinowski, eds. *Youth Crime, Social Control and Prevention: Theoretical Perspectives and Policy Implications*. Pfaffenweiler, Germany: Centaurus-Verlagsgesellschaft. *Bundeskriminalamt*. 1989. *Polizeiliche Kriminalstatistik*, 1988. Weisbaden: Kriminalistisches Institut.

Calico, David. 1978. *The German Problem Reconsidered: Germany and the World Order, 1870 to the Present*. Cambridge. England: Cambridge University Press. Chandler, William M. and Alan Siarnoff. 1986. Postindustrial Politics in Germany and the Origins of the Greens. *Comparative Politics* 18 (3), 303-322.

Cook, Chris and John Paxton. 1986. *European Political Facts*, 1918-84. New York: Facts on File, Inc.

Cooper, Belinda (1996) "The Fall of the Wall and the East German Police," in *Policing in Central and Eastern Europe: Comparing Firsthand Knowledge with Experience from the West*, Milan Pagon, Editor, Ljubljana, Slovenia: College of Police and Security Studies.

Craig, Gordon A. 1978. *Germany, 1866-1945*. New York: Oxford University Press.

Dahrendorf, Roif. 1967. *Society and Democracy*. New York: Doubleday & Company.

Edsworth, Raymond. 1960. *Restoring Democracy in Germany*. London: Stevens & Sons Ltd.

Edinger, Lewis J. 1986. *West German Politics*. New York: Columbia University Press.

Fairchild, Erika S. 1990. The Uses of Research: Politics, Academics, and the Police in the United States of America and the Federal Republic of Germany. *Criminal Justice Review 15 (1)*, 5-12.

1988. German Police: Ideals and Reality in the Post War Years. Springfield, IL: Charles C. Thomas.

1984. Demilitarization of Police Forces: The Case of the Federal Republic of Germany. *Police Studies* 7 (4) 189-200.

Feltes, Thomas R. 1988. The Function and the Role of the Police in the Federal Republic of Germany. A paper presented at the Annual Meeting of the American Society of Criminology in Chicago.

1988. Personal Interview, Chicago.

Fogelson, Robert M. 1977. *Big-City Police*. Cambridge, MA: Harvard University Press.

Fosdick, Raymond R. 1915. *European Police System*. London: George Allen & Unwin, Ltd.

Fowler, Norman. 1979. *After the Riots: the Police in Europe*. London: Davis Poynter Limited.

Gaugler, Eduard. 1990. The Structure of and Institution for Business Administration in German-Speaking Countries. In Erwin Grochla and Eduard Gaugler, eds. *Handbook of German Business Management*. Stuttgart: C.E Poeschel (Springer Verlag).

Gellately, Robert. 1990. *The Gestapo and German Society.* Oxford, England: Clarendon Press.

Gemmer, Karl-Heinz. 1988. Personal Correspondence.

Gramckow, Heike (1995) "The Influence of History and the Rule of Law on the Development of Community Policing in Germany," *Police Studies,* Volume 18, No. 2.

1978. Police and Crime-Control in the Federal Republic of Germany. *Police Studies* 1(1), *55-6* 1.

Giles, Geoffrey J. 1985. *Students and National Socialism in Germany.* Princeton, NJ: Princeton University Press.

Gold, Raymond L. 1970. Roles in Sociological Field Observations. In Norman K. Denzin, ed. *Sociological Methods.* Chicago: Aldine Publishing Company.

Haggkvist, Gart. 1988. Personal Interview. Vaasa, Finland.

Heiland, Hans-Gunther, 1992. Modern Patterns of Crime and Control in the Federal Republic of Germany. In Hans-Gunther Heiland, Louise I. Shelley and Hisao Katoh Gemmer, KarlHeinz, eds. *Crime and Control in Comparative Perspectives.* New York, Berlin: Walter do Gruyter.

Herrmann, Joachim. 1984. Federal Republic of Germany. In George F. Cole, Stanislaw J. Frankowski and Marc G. Gertz, eds. *Major Criminal Justice System.* Beverly Hills, CA: Sage Publictations.

Hucko, Elmar M. 1989. *The Democratic Tradition.* New York: Berg Publishers Limited.

Jager, Joachim. 1984. Assaults on German Police Officers. *Police Studies* 6 (4), 18-21.

Johnson, Nevil. 1983. State and Government in the Federal Republic of Germany. New York: Pergamon Press.

Kasti, Gerhard, 1982. Task Force Police. *IPA-Weltkongress.* Wiesbaden: Germany.

Katzenstein, Peter J. 1987. *Policy and Politics in West Germany: The Growth of a Semi-Sovereign State.* Philadelphia: Temple University Press.

Klonz, Barbara. 1990. Personal Interview. Hamburg.

Koetzsche, Helmut. 1987. Providing Police Services That Better Serve the Public. *Police Studies* 10(4), 172-180.

Kratz, Gunter. 1986. Personal Interview. Munster.

Kube, Edwin 1997. "Pro-Active Policing in Germany," *EuroCriminology*, Vol 11.

1984. Tasks and Functions of the Polizei-Führungsakademie of the Federal Republic of Germany. *Police Studies* 7 (1), 49-57.

1980. PFA *Studienplan*. Muster: Polizeifuhrungasakademie.

Kube, Edwin. 1982. Narcotics and Crime Prevention. *Police Studies* 5 (1), 14-18.

Laitinen, Ahti. 1988. Personal Interview. Turku.

Lane, Jan-Erik and Svante O. Ersson. 1977. *Politics and Society in Western Europe*. Beverly Hills, CA: Sage Publications Ltd.

Lofland, John, 1984. *Analyzing Social Settings*. Belmont, CA: Wadsworth Publishing.

Lohndorf, B. 1990. Personal Interview, Hamburg.

1973. The National Advisory Commission on Criminal Justice Standards and Goals. *Police.* Washington D.C.: Government Printing Office.

Nebelin, Lutz. 1982. Der Bundesgrenzschutz (Federal Border Guard), The Federal Police. *IPAWeltkongress*. Weisbaden: Germany.

Palmer, Geoffrey. 1986. The Legislative Process and the Police. In Cameron Neil and Warren Young, eds. *Policing at Crossroad*. Wellington: Port Nicholas Press.

Reise, Peter. 1990. Personal Interview, Hamburg.

Ruckrigel, Werner. 1986. Police Operations at Demonstrations. *Police Studies* 9 (3), 148-150.

Schmidt, Helmut. 1989. *Men and Powers*. New York: Random House.

Sessar, Klaus, 1991. *Research in* Criminology. New York: Springer Verlag.

Steven, James W. 1983. Basic and Advanced Training of Police Officers: A Comparison of West Germany and the United States. *Police Studies* 6 (3), 24-35.

Tanner, Raimo. 1988. Personal Interview, Tampere, Finland.

Thomaneck, Jurgen. 1985. Police and Public Order in the Federal Republic of Germany. In John Roach and Jurgen Thomaneck eds. *Police and Public Order in Europe.* London: Crook Helm.

Von Kock, Alexander. 1979. Police Consolidation in Germany. *The Police Chief 46 (9),* 46-48.

The Wall Street Journal, January 26, 1989, A1O.

Wundered, Roif. 1990 Leadership. In Erwin Grochia and Eduard Gaugler, eds. *Handbook of German Business Management.* Stuttgart: C.E. Poeschel (Springer Verlag).

Ziegler, Herbest F. 1989. *Nazi Germany's New Aristocracy.* Princeton, New Jersey: Princeton University Press.

Chapter 5

Uprightness and Bureaucratic
Conformity
The Finnish Police

Introduction

During his study of the Finnish police the overarching note that the observing author could ascribe to the police in Finland was that they exude a clear spirit of uprightness, just and straightforward character but also an unmistakable adherence to the rules which one may describe as bureaucratic procedures. In this chapter on the police of Finland with an account of their organizational structure, training and education, search for simplification and certitudes, conventional views on police work, stress on this theme as the recurring feature of the police in Finland will be pursued.

The observer author was impressed by the straightforward responses to the questions during interviews. Some of the responses were as follows: Police officers said that they enjoyed working in the streets as roving peace officers without being supervised. As Finns, patrol officers say, they were sensitive to supervision, they trusted their superiors and would like to be trusted by them in return. Their performances, they were glad, were not measured in terms of tickets, arrests, citations, and other such criteria. The Finnish officers were proud and upright. However, they were also capable of laughing at themselves, their bureaucratic rule and regulation. The law required that police officers in Finland worked in pairs; it was necessary for collaboration of evidence in court. However, they said that this rule had made them a laughing stock in society. People said that the police always worked in pairs, because one could only read and there must be another with him who could write.

Historical Background Information

The country of Finland is one of five Scandinavian countries that consist of Denmark, Iceland, Norway, and Sweden. The Scandinavian countries are fairly similar to each other in social and political systems. Finland is one of the largest countries in Europe with 338,145 sq. kilometers. However, the population density of the country is low. The majority of the people belong to the Lutheran Church, the official church of the country (Laitinen, 1994).

Five million people live in Finland and except for some Gypsies and a few foreigners, including those admitted to the country since 1985, the people are Finnish. In 1999, there were 17,623 refugees in Finland. Singleton (1989) claims, "approximately 90 percent of the Finnish population is still Lutheran and white." Although "some ethnic minorities exist," the country "has never been in a position to allow the relatively open door migration policies which have enriched the national cultures of such countries as Britain, Germany and the United States." Solsten and Meditz add that the country has been "on Europe's periphery, both physically and socially, for almost all its history." It is "a remarkably homogeneous country" with no "racial minorities." During 1990s, small racial minorities have begun to develop along with the increasing number of refugees: for example the Vietnamese and the Somalia's refugees along with the gypsies who have formed a racial minority for decades. The largest minority, the Swedish-speaking Finns, are "so well assimilated with the majority that there were fears they would eventually disappear.

"The Lapps or *Sami*, an ethnic group, live in the northern most part of Finland and are the "oldest known inhabitants of the country." The approximately 5,000 Lapps, like Finns, speak a language "belonging to the Fenno-Ugric family of languages." The Gypsies have been in Finland since "the second half of the sixteenth century," and there are approximately 6,000 of them. Cultural homogeneity is matched by Finland's "relative absence of class distinctions" in social and public life (Sinngleton, 1989).

Finns speak a language known as *Suomi* which belongs to the uralic group of languages spoken in Northeastern Europe, Western Siberia, and Hungary. Wuorinen (1965) states that the Finnish language "differs greatly from the other languages of Europe." However, "the exceptional isolation of the Finnish race" has not avoided "an intermixture" which results from "thousands of years of migrations, wars and peaceful intercourse." Pentikainen and Anttonen (1985) remark that "there has been a continuous misconception of Finnish society as being a homogeneous whole." Although isolation and homogeneity lend a special characteristic to Finland, Allardt (1985) describes Finland as "connected with the vast land masses of Eurasia, and throughout history" it has "always had an extensive border with Russia." Finland is a "Nordic" society, very much like Swedish society particularly due to "her being part of the Swedish realm from the Middle Ages up to 1809." Following the 1808-1809 war, Finland was ceded by Sweden to Russia as a "Grand Duchy" with the Czar as the country's "Grand Duke". Consequently, "the autonomous Grand Duchy of Finland inherited from Sweden a framework of jurisdiction and the laws of Sweden." Alapuro (1980) refers to "two central characteristics in the formation of the Finnish nation." Finland was "consolidated in a territory between two established members of the European state system," and "the Finnish state developed in the interface between two centers, Sweden and Russia." Finland's Nordic neighbor, Sweden, was "economically and culturally dominant," while Russia's influence was "politically dominant but economically backward."

Two years after Finland declared its independence from Russia, a constitution was adopted in 1919. According to the constitution, Finland is a bilingual state and all administrative work, higher education, and police schooling are conducted in Finnish and Swedish. Allardt (1985) elaborates:

> There are elements from Eastern Europe and the Baltic countries in Finnish culture, and the country's culture has been stimulated by

many impulses from other countries mainly, for a long period of time, from Germany. In many respects, Finland has been a melting pot for separate Finnish, Swedish-Nordic, East European-Baltic and southern, mainly German, cultural element

After independence, Finland faced a cruel civil war between the Reds and Whites, consisting of industrial and agricultural workers with Bolshevik orientations and the Whites, composed of land-owning peasants and led by Carl Mannerheim. Germany helped Finland's Whites, who were government troops, route the Reds and prevented Finland's "absorption into the Soviet Union" (Jutikkala, 1962). Nousiainen (1971) notes that:

> After the war had ended, in the spring of 1918, it became clear that supporters of a monarchy had increased their strength considerably; two proposals for a monarchy were made ... the German Prince Friedrich Karl of Hessen was proclaimed the King of Finland.

Maude (1976) wrote that "a large section of the Finnish educated class was actually drawn to Germany." According to Sinisalo (1971), "the juridical literature ... has been influenced by Germany." The prolonged and rigorous "education" of police officers of all ranks seems to be designed after the German model.

In Finland with its "multiplicity of political parties, the tendency of their political groupings is to become more heterogeneous both ideologically and in social structure" (Pesonen and Rantala, 1985). However, the "extreme and polarized multi-party system" has been characterized since the 1960s by "a consensual style of decision-making." Seppo Randell, senior professor of sociology (1990) at the University of Tampere, observed that cultural homogeneity has been matched recently by the politics of consensus.

In the early 1950s Finland's economy was "highly agriculture-dominated," but by 1980, "the share of agricultural population ... decreased to 13 percent of the economically active population" with a simultaneous increase in "both the industrial and service sectors." Compared to France, England and

Sweden, the Finnish socio-economic situation "reflects late industrialization" (Alestalo, Andorka, and Harcsa, 1987). In 2000, the share of agricultural population has decreased to 7.4% (MARE-project of the Ministry of Labor) and the trend is further decreasing. Vartola (1988) calls the present administrative and political situation "a state of equilibrium." In contemporary Finland "great social or political conflicts" are absent:

> In the prevailing stable situation the leading government parties and the most influential interest groups are living in peaceful co-existence. In terms of administration, the implication of the stable situation is that long-pending projects for the reform of administration are at a standstill.

The governmental structure of Finland consists of 5 provinces. There were 12 providences until this was changed in January 1997. There are 448 municipalities divided into urban municipalities and rural municipalities.

Research methodology

The observer author began his study of the Finnish police in Turku, a city of historic importance in Finland. Under the innovative leadership of Chief Juhani Salonen, Turku Police are known throughout the Scandinavia as having the most imaginative community policing experiments. With the guidance of Chief Salonen and his Community Police Deputy, *Komisario* (Chief Inspector) Kalevi Salonen, a number of police jurisdictions in the entire country were studied.

These include old city police departments in Helsinki, Tampere, Hamina, Vaasa, Jyvaskyla, and Tornio. Also studied were so-called new city police headed by sheriffs, called *Nimismies,* in Espoo, Rovaniemi, Kouvola as well as in many distant locations in Virolahti, Kitee, Joensuu, Ilomantsi, Salla, Kemio, Inari, and Ylitornio. The observer author spent time in Maarianhamina, the capital city of the Swedish-speaking autonomous region administered by Finland (the province of Åland (Ahvenanmaa) forms an independent police district). Today, there are 90 local police departments operating under the five Provincial Police Command

Offices. One police department may have offices in several locations.

The study of the Finnish police allowed the observer-author to participate in police work, particularly on street patrols conducted by the police and on organized traffic checks by the Finnish Mobile Police (the police use the translation Traffic Police) or *Liikkuva Poliisi*. During this study, in-depth interviews with police officers of all ranks who seemed willing to talk were conducted by the observer author. Among approximately 200 officers who were interviewed, there were English-speaking officers who were directly interviewed; in addition to those who were interviewed through interpreters. Interviews were conducted on the basis of a questionnaire designed to elicit police opinions on police work, police officers' perception of their environment, their pride, power, and deviance, and organizational changes they would welcome. As indicated above, the observer author also gathered evidence of what struck him as the dominant note in characterizing the Finnish police: uprightness and bureaucratic conformity.

Police structure: traditional and bureaucratic

Finland has a centralized police structure located at the headquarters at the Ministry of the Interior. The police structure is headed by one *General Director, National Police Commissioner*, assisted by high-ranking officers. The centralized organization of the police was partly due to the long Russian hegemony over Finland (Torke, 1989). Historically "the municipal Finnish police gradually became a state police when Finland was annexed to Russia in 1809" (Rautkallio, 1988). In a prominent place in the Mikkeli police station, a visitor can see the declaration of the establishment of the police department by the Czar:

> On December 31 of 1903 His Majesty the Emperor graciously decreed that a complete police department be established in the city of Mikkeli. This decree assigned for the new police department nineteen employees, namely, one Komisario (Chief Inspector), two Senior Constables and fourteen Constables. Among these the Senior Constable and one Constable in upper salary

category were ordered to serve in the capacity of Detective Policemen.

Designations, prevalent during the Czarist regime, like *poliisimestari* (this title is not used any more in service), *sihteeri, komisario, ylikonstaapeli* and *konstaapeli* are still used. The higher status of detectives whose rank designations are preceded by the honorific, rikos (direct translation of 'rikos' is crime or criminal, but it is often translated as detective as in detective sergeant - rikosylikonstaapeli) was granted in the Czar's time. In the Mikkeli station the visitor will see that until 1917 the chiefs at the station were army officers from the emperor's army. From 1917 to 1921, chiefs came from the Finnish army. In 1921 a person educated in law became the chief. In 1941 a promoted chief was appointed, and when he retired in 1971, another man was promoted to chief from among the police personnel at the station. Such promotions are rare in Finland's Police, because most chiefs come from university law schools.

The Finnish administration culture, which affects the national police, continues to be dominated by its Russian bureaucratic heritage. A government publication (1987) states that "the administrative machinery has not adjusted well to the needs of the welfare state ... administration has not sufficiently been able to serve its clients." The report suggests efforts for "the improvement of the quality of services" including "planning and coordination," "leadership," "staff policies," and "many other procedures that do not meet the requirements set for modern administration." In 1997 the Providence Reform took place along with the reform of the jurisdictional districts.

In Finland the police are a part of the state administration with this agency being nationalized. The organization, functions, duties and rights of the police are prescribed in the Police Act of 1995 and Police Law of 1995. The Minister of the Interior oversees all police operations. Under the Minister of the Interior is the National Police Commissioner who is the administrator of all police in Finland. Under the Department of Police Affairs there are four bureaus:

179

1. Management Unit
2. Police Unit
3. Administrative Unit
4. Information Unit

The Technical Bureau has been abolished and a new Police Data Administration Center has been established to work as an independent bureau housed at the National Bureau of Investigation.

There are several units under the Department of Police Affairs that have various duties and responsibilities. For example, the Police School and Police College have the responsibility of police training which will discussed later in this chapter. The Police Dog Institute has the duty of acquiring police dogs and their training. The Police Storage Depots are responsible for firearms, automobiles, information systems and other equipment (Laitinen, 1994).

Under the Minister of the Interior three police bureaus operate directly under the Supreme Police Command. They are the National Bureau of Investigation (NBI), the Traffic Police Department and the Security Police. NBI has a national office in Vantaa and twelve regional bureaus around the country located in major cities. Investigative personnel are recruited from other police departments. Generally, the investigators come from the detective ranks at the local police department level. Crimes are typically investigated initially at the local level by local police officers with the more difficult cases given to the NBI (Parker, 1993).

The National Traffic Police, was created in 1930 under the Ministry of the Interior. The department was organized to operate throughout the country with the purpose to prevent smuggling, control traffic movements, and to suppress civil disturbances. The law that governs the Traffic Police requires that they must assist other police departments, maintain public order, and safety, engage in crime prevention and traffic control. In addition, the Traffic Police function as a national police reserve (Parker, 1993). The law pertaining to the

Mobile Police divides the duties into four categories (Parker, 1993):

1. The control, organization and guidance of land traffic, as well as traffic education and research;

2. The prevention of the illegal importation of alcoholic beverages, and their unauthorized manufacture, transport, or sales;

3. The supervision of water traffic, hunting, fishing, and nature conservation;

4. Assisting other police units in searches and investigations and in capturing fugitives from justice.

In 1948, the Security Police was created under the Minister of the Interior. It was mandated to solve crimes against the state. These crimes include terrorist acts and bank robberies (Parker, 1993).

The National Commissioner of the Police is the operational head of the police forces in Finland. There are 90 local districts within Finland. Each of the districts has a police chief as head. A provincial police commissioner heads every regional administration (Joutsen and Lahti, 1997).

The Finland police cannot infringe upon the individual rights of citizens except when expressly allowed by Finnish law. The right to use force by the police is permitted only when they meet resistance while performing their duties. The amount of force used can be no greater than is necessary to perform the duty. The Police Act provides detailed requirements on prevention measures, such as when the police can confiscate dangerous objectives. The Finnish police are guided by the Police Act, which regulates the surveillance of individuals. Under the Finnish police system the exercise of police powers, which includes the use of force, is subject to close supervision by senior police officials, the Ombudsman of Parliament and the Chancellor of Justice (Joutsen and Lahti, 1997).

The Police Law renewed in 1995, the Police Act of 1995, defines police authority. The Police Law § 1 states that "the task of the police is to protect the legal and social order, to maintain public order and security, to prevent and investigate crimes and to bring them under consideration of charges." Uusitalo, Professor of the Sociology of Law at the University of Helsinki and a police researcher (1990), claims that no attempt has been made to change the historically narrow role of Finnish police as security agents of the state. He added that society has not felt the need to expand the role of the police, because Finland is a welfare state, and law and order in it has been maintained. In another context Uusitalo (1983) adds that Finland has "the strictest criminal policy" which is responsible for the "remarkably higher number of prisoners" in this country than in other Scandinavian countries. Finnish police work in a climate that is marked by "deep rooted legalism." Little conflict exists between the police and civilian groups, and the country has not experienced "any potentially violent confrontation between labor and capital" since 1956. The student activism of the 1960s "never developed to the degree of violent confrontation," and like other Scandinavian countries, the level of violence in confrontations is "low" in Finland. Uusitalo explains that Finland is unique in that civil disobedience has occupied "an important role in the Finnish national mythology," and it has prevented "the dogmatic licence for law and order rhetoric even in the very conservative sections of the society." Uusitalo remarks that "as civil servants, the Finnish police are also influenced by the same national mythology." He comments:

> The Cabinets are normally coalitions of several political groups. Compromising inside the cabinet is inevitable in Finnish policy.. .The Finnish police are probably more bound by the conflicting webs of political connections in the administration and in the political system than any other police force in Scandinavia. ..The police may feel that the political control is more effective in Finland than is some other Scandinavian countries for organizational reasons. They are under the direct control of the Ministry of the Interior without any independent police central organization.

Finland is a peaceful country, because crime in general (Joutsen, 1989) is well under control. It is a matter of satisfaction to the police that "in comparison with other Nordic countries, criminality in Finland is not very high" (National Institute of Legal Policy, 1988). In the long run, the number of reported crimes has increased: In 1950, 51,000 crimes violating the Penal Code were reported, in 1997, the number was 370,000 (Crime and Criminal Justice in Finland 1997, National Institute of Legal Policy). The police are viewed as doing an effective job. They take pride that "Finland, as compared with Norway, has a clearance rate that has been twice as high ... almost no waivers of prosecution are used...Finland has the largest number of prisoners in the Nordic countries" (Balvig, 1985). In the early twenty-first century, the detention may last for three days, after that a court consideration is required. The court can allocate two weeks detention at a time, a new consideration is required once in every two weeks. In a number of cities, the surveillance of public movement, particularly young peoples' activities, is accomplished with cameras installed at strategic downtown locations. An opinion survey (1988) indicated that the public considered the surveillance a "positive development." In support of bureaucratic conformity of the Finnish police one can refer to the Russian tradition, centralized police structure and deep rooted legalism and so on.

Elaborate and structured police training

In Finland police training is very elaborate. The Finns refer to training as *Koulutus* or education. Tapani Valkonen (1990), who headed the Sociology Department at the University of Helsinki, mentioned that education was so important that Finns had been electing only famous constitutional lawyers or persons with doctorate degrees as Presidents of Finland including the present one. The present President, Tarja Halonen, is a lawyer but the one before her, Martti Ahtisaari, was a teacher. According to Alkio et al. (1988), "some 30,000 Finns ... 1.3 percent of the work force are retrained each year ... the average length of employment courses is six months." They add "labor authorities buy training from the vocational course centers, vocational schools and institutions of higher education subordinate to the Ministry of Education." Prosecutors (Joutsen and Kalske, 1984) in Finland attend "two week prosecutor refresher courses each year."

The Municipal Training Institute provides "supplementary and further training for elected and appointed municipal officials, in addition to basic training in municipal affairs for appointed officials" (1983), with 175 courses conducted annually. Vartola (1988) mentions that the number of civil servants with "academic education rose in the period 1950-1975 for 27 to 43 percent." He also notes "a general raising of the level of training." A high level commission established in 1986 by the Finnish government to improve civil administration suggested (Venna, 1989) that in the 1990s "an intensive and effective training program for the central administration as well as for local governments" should be established. In the annual reports of the Parliamentary Ombudsman in 1984, 1985 and 1986, suggestions were offered for improving police training in order to avoid public complaints. A report from the Tampere Police Department states (1987) that it "spent a total of 263 days in special classes with 101 members participating." A booklet (1989) published by the Helsinki Police Department describes various training programs arranged for its personnel, including the people working at the police garage. The National Bureau of Investigation describes its training efforts (1987) as follows:

> Our personnel had training to a considerable extent. The training in The use of microscope-photometer took place in *Bundeskriminalamt* in the Federal Republic of Germany. The training in FTIR-spectrophotometry was given in London. Elsewhere in England our personnel got training from the manufacturers of electronic microscopes...; to some extent in Holland and in Sweden, the country of import. Additional chances to become familiar with the electronic microscope occurred in Norway.

The Turku Police Department has established a "Justice Education Work Group" for planning annual seminars "meant for police, teachers, social workers and youth workers" (1988). This department also conducts on behalf of the Turku Summer University a course entitled, "Narcotics, Intoxicants and Today's Youth," for school nurses, police officers who teach justice education classes to school children, school counselors, school welfare officers and youth welfare officers. Concerning the Project to Improve Pre-Trial Investigation which would reduce the police powers of detention and prolonged investigations, great faith in police training is described (1987):

> Our Committee ... suggests that a "rush order" be issued for the construction of the buildings for the Police School in Tampere. More training programs will be needed because of the new pre-trial investigation law and all statutes attached to it. Also, we will soon have a revision of the crime law. Any temporary improvement will help momentarily and therefore, we need to plan for the future.

In Finland the police are educated at the Police School in Tampere and at the Police College in Otaniemi. The Police School received a new building in the early 1990s, and the Police Academy was given the status of vocational high school, ammattikorkeakoulu, in the latter half of the 1990s. The former is for basic recruiting, and the latter is attended by sergeants or *Ylikonstaapeli* and Chief Inspectors or *Komisario*. In fact, Police School is now at the level of *Opistoaste* (technical school) and Police College is *ammattikorkeakoulu*, (vocational high school). The Ministry of the Interior states:

> The Secondary Education Development Act (474/78) has been the basis of the development of police training...the basic and advanced training of policemen has to be renovated in such a way that the training will be comparable to the vocational training subordinate to the National Board of Vocational Education and also that the training can be drawn upon in continued studies when applicable. According to these principles, the police department has made a plan for adapting the basic and advanced training of policemen to the secondary education development ... A policeman who has passed the policeman's basic examination can seek admission to a suitable university program. Studies in the police field can to a certain extent be drawn upon in university studies. NOW it is possible to continue from the Police College to the University of Turku or University of Tampere, and many chief

inspectors have already graduated.

Recruits at the Police School are regarded as students. Their minimum educational qualifications can be earned at a senior high school or a vocational school or institute. They must have completed a period of compulsory military training, (if male), achieving at least the rank of a non-commissioned officer. They must have been found suitable by the Police Selection Board consisting of the Police School Headmaster, other instructors, some police as well as non-police. They must have a "life style, health and personality suitable for police work" (1988). However, on the island of Ahvenanmaa, the autonomous, Swedish-speaking province in Finland, the local police department is allowed to hire its own police officers. Police students can apply for government loans to study at the Police School, although they are offered free accommodations and board during the period of their training. The competition for entry is extreme, and approximately three hundred students are accepted every year from a pool of 4,000 applicants (1988). For example, during the period of December 1, 1997, and November 30, 1998, there were 2649 applicants and only 312 were accepted.

Basic police basic training consists of 108 credits, and it takes about two years and four months to complete the program. The first part consists of eighty credits of basic studies; twenty credits are supervised practical training. The second part consists of twenty-eight credits of advanced professional studies that consist of lessons on basic police work (nine credits), crime prevention (eight credits), six months of field work (six credits) and a final essay (five credits).

The Police College is for the education of commissioned officers, Sergeants or *Ylikonstaapeli* and chief inspectors or *Komisario.* The former are educated for twenty-five credits that can be finished during two to three years (from 1993 to 1998 the studies consisted of twenty credits). The latter are educated for three-and-one-half years for 120 credits. The preceding educational institution is a vocational high school that is situated somewhere between former technical schools (opistoaste) and universities. Like the Police School, the College is the final authority in deciding who should enter the institution to be educated for the promotions to the ranks of sergeant and lieutenant. The selection procedure is as follows (1987):

> The Director of the Police *Academy* (Currently, translated as Police College) invites a sufficient number of the applicants to an entrance examination. His invitations are based on recommendations of the Selection Committee. The Committee selects those candidates who ... fulfill the requirements.

The number of women in training is relatively low. The primary reason for this has been that women were not allowed to join the police until 1973. Between 1973 and 1975 there were only 53 positions for women. Eventually the 53 slots were expanded to 180 police positions, which than constituted 2.2 percent of all police officers. In Commanding officers training the representation of females has been minimal. With the passage of the Act for Equal Rights for Men and Women in 1987 the recruitment of women has received an impetus (Laitinen, 1994).

The College also has three different merit scholarship programs. They have an Alumni Association for "the purpose of cultural and social endeavors of the present and earlier class members." It has a student government "to promote ways of spending leisure time, and to initiate actions on questions that concern students." It uses a large number of lecturers (500 in 1987) from outside the academy. Thus, the police of Finland, like the nation as a whole, are religiously committed to elaborate and serious professional training.

Stress on simplification and certitudes

In Finland law courses are extensive and thorough, but constitutional law is not included in them. In the Finnish constitution one finds rules of guidance for all other laws made in the country. As Lehtimaja (1977) remarks, "the protection of the fundamental rights of the citizens in the context of criminal proceedings has seldom been treated as a question of constitutional law ... unlike in the United States, constitutional issues are only seldom raised at court level. In Finland "the

187

principle of equality before law is highly valued" (Tornudd, 1968), and training in law is marked by an emphasis on practicality. Generally in teaching law to police officers, it is considered necessary to emphasize the practical impact of the legal rules; abstract legal principles have little use in street work as mentioned to the observer author by the instructors at the Police School who echoed a police researcher in the USA (Skolnick, 1975).

Human relations were said to be permeating every aspect of police training at the Tampere Police School, and it is, therefore, difficult to assess the extent of human relations training on the basis of the specific courses and the hours allocated to them. The courses on psychology do not include instruction on community relations or race and minority relations. Because Finland is almost entirely a homogeneous country, the army, the judicial system, and the national police organization form the "traditional core" (Tiihonen, 1989) of bureaucracy, and "the present day administrative units do carry traces of age-old ties." "The central administration created in Finland at the beginning of the period of autonomy ... was felt to be a danger due to Russian unification tendencies." In a Government of Finland publication (1987), it has been mentioned that "in everyday functioning of the administration negative bureaucratic features become apparent." Cultural and racial homogeneity as well as the traditional nature of the Finnish bureaucracy probably explains why community relations type courses are conspicuous by their absence in the police human relations training program.

In Finland a discussion of police subculture is not included in ethics, because subculture is not considered a problem, according to the ethics instructor (Valitalo, 1990). Moreover, there is no body of literature on police subculture in Finland. Judges all over the country said that the standard of police investigation is high. Most police officers maintain that they enjoy considerable public respect and feel proud of their occupation. In Finland all police departments employ civilians for handling miscellaneous administrative responsibilities like issuing passports, and as a result, the departments are not manned exclusively by police officers. Moreover, chiefs of police departments are often law graduates from universities without formal police training. In rural police departments, police employees who work as prosecutors are also lawyers, but not always. Because civilians, law graduates, and lawyers are part of Finnish police, a police subculture is unlikely to form according to police officers, judges, and university professor in that country.

Police perception of their work: Conventional views

Most officers seemed to like their job specialization as uniformed police, detectives, local traffic police or as members of national police agencies like the Traffic Police, NBI and the Security Police. Some thought that Finnish police should develop increased specialization in organized crime, drug offenses, computer fraud, and economic offenses. The division of labor and specialization between uniformed police and detectives is clear in every police department. Also the detectives in the biggest police departments have specialized in different types of crime, for example, drugs, white-collar crime, and property crimes. In 1993, regional centers for crime investigations which concentrated on the most serious types of crimes were established in Finland. Asked whether law enforcement, peacekeeping, or social service appealed to them most, the police officers gave a variety of responses. Generally, detectives preferred law enforcement, and uniformed police preferred peacekeeping. Patrol officers in America prefer peacekeeping, because they consider arrest a hassle (Wilson, 1978), but Finnish officers considered peace keeping a two-fold blessing. The Finnish police officers maintained that by keeping the peace they were fulfilling their role as well as helping people avoid the consequences of arrest and prosecution. Some sheriffs with law enforcement, prosecution and, distrainer responsibilities and some Traffic *Police* officers (*Liikkuva Poliisi*) who enforced traffic regulations also preferred peacekeeping. Personnel in community police work in Turku seemed to prefer all aspects of police work. They confirmed the San Diego Community Police findings that community policing was psychologically rewarding to police officers, because they became involved in

189

every aspect of the job (Boydstun and Sherry, 1975). Mantila (1988) has noted the variety of work entailed in *Korttelipoliisi* or community policing, like "patrolling on foot or bike, visits to and presentations at different meetings and events." They gave speeches at schools "on traffic and law." They provided "various types of information" and rode in "car patrols." The community police officers believed that their work was "productive," that the areas within their control "had become more peaceful," and that their level of satisfaction was "linked with a readiness to help private citizens with their problems and engage in long-term preventive work."

Few officers preferred the social service aspects of police work, and for the national police institution in Finland, it is not easy to become involved in social services. A report on the experience of "the first co-operational experiment between the police and social workers in cases of domestic violence" (1985) stated:

> The police work and its expenses belong to the domain of the state. Social work with its expenses, as far as it concerns such special assignments, is a responsibility of the municipality or of a special private organization paid by the town. For such reasons, the allocation of these tasks to one police unit will be a legal as well as practical problem in regard to the concept of police duty as understood by the personnel, their training priorities, and in the sharing of expenses.

The report also states "the line between police work and social work may lose its distinction."

Most calls received at the "Alarm Centre" or the police control room in Helsinki were about removing drunkards or stopping noisy youth parties. In 2000, there was a public discussion initiated by the police whether removing drunkards should be the duty of the police or if it was to be shifted to social workers. In India, Israel, the Netherlands, and England (Shane, 1980), the police are primarily engaged in social services. Finland is "a highly developed industrial or post-industrial welfare state" (Kuisma, 1989), "a Northern welfare state" (Alestalo, Flora, Uusitalo, 1985) with well-organized social services. The Helsinki Police

190

Department (1989) has found that at their control room "the total number of registered tasks annually is nearly 130,000. Out of these, 4,000 are calls reporting assaults, 16,000 crimes against property, 12,000 domestic disturbances, 7,300 traffic accidents, 4,000 drunk drivers, and 37,000 intoxicated people. The rest of the calls were miscellaneous "alarms." According to a report (1989), the "proportions of the various types of alarm calls" in Helsinki to the country as a whole are: 25.4 percent drunkenness, 8.8 percent traffic accidents, 4.3 percent traffic tasks, 5.1 percent thefts, 6.7 percent domestic disputes, 18.6 percent calls for police help and 31.1 percent miscellaneous calls. Police officers on their rounds of duty intervened mostly in situations involving public drunkenness, noisy parties by youngsters, domestic disputes, unsafe driving; they did not receive many calls for social services. Police officers said that Finland was a welfare state with a variety of free social services, and consequently, the police were not needed for social services.

Supervisors are expected to be more experienced, better informed and more accountable than the officers subordinate to them. Supervision does not need to be meddling, disruptive, and detrimental to the development of initiative in junior officers (Punch, 1983). Supervisors with the rank of *komisario* or chief inspector said that Finns generally resented supervision. Therefore, police supervisors were very discreet and circumspect in supervising personnel. The absence of strict supervision seemed satisfying at the Police School, i.e., Police School in Tampere, where candidates in the pre-service training compared their compulsory time in the army with the relaxed and pleasant climate at the police school. Police chiefs and rural police chiefs also claimed that the most satisfactory aspect of their jobs was that the Provincial Police or *Laaninpoliisitarkastaja* was not in a position to interfere in their day-to-day activities.

A policy based on respect for individual autonomy and freedom seemed to be an objective pursued by the government in all civil service. Venna (1989) states that the Finnish civil administration emphasizes "trust and openness, more freedom in implementation, personal growth and self-control." Vartola (1988)

191

notes that department heads are "the chiefs in the different areas," and "delegating actually does occur to a large extent." Sinisalo (1971) mentions that "the Ministry of Interior has had since 1935 the power to give police orders but that power has not been used." Regarding the independence enjoyed by the departments in the central government, Nousiainen (1971) observes that they are characterized by "a detachment and independence." The departments have "a well developed pyramidical organization that includes the key position of the department head, and extensive decision-making power," including "the police department within the Ministry of the Interior." The practice of administrative autonomy and leaving people to themselves (Singleton, 1989) seems in Finland to consist of "the relative absence of those invisible social barriers which seem to inhibit the full development of the human spirit," "the relative absence of class distinctions in education, in everyday social life and in the protocols of public life," and in the "pragmatism of taking people as one finds them." Kirby (1990) mentions that "the classic working class of urbanized industrialized Western Europe has never featured prominently in Finnish life."

Patrol work can be boring and monotonous (Van Maanen, 1978), but most officers do not mention the monotony of their work. Patrol officers are quite enthusiastic in talking about the variety and novelty in their otherwise routine existence on the streets.

The complaint of too much work is mainly voiced by people in senior positions. The pressures of day-to-day work are time consuming and do not allow senior officers to have time to think and reflect as they should (Goldstein, 1977). Field officers of senior status were frustrated, because they were unable to see the busy superior police officers stationed at the Ministry of the Interior. Skolnick and Bayley (1986) suggest that the new breed of police are "thinkers rather than shooters," and the "intellectual" police leaders like Brown of Houston have been responsible for policing innovation. Working in Finland seems to leave no room for thinking police leaders.

During the time of research police shifts were rotated every three weeks.

192

Some shifts seemed unusually long, and rotations appeared frequent. Some officers found shift work disruptive of family and social relationships and also physically exhausting. They also stressed that extra long holidays following continuous work helped remove the traces of wear and tear. Some personnel at the lowest levels felt that there could be more consultations between management and employees in regard to shift allotments.

Quite a few officers in patrol work felt that they did not have enough protection against the hazards of their jobs. They regretted that bullet-proof vests, which were available at departments, were not issued personally. They felt that guns which were officially issued were not sophisticated, and that too many restrictions existed on the use of guns for genuine self-defense. Some younger officers also felt that a few practices were against security principles. One officer in the Traffic Police or *Liikkuva Poliisi* felt that the present practice of allowing a traffic offender to sit inside a patrol car while writing a ticket was frightening, because the offender could be armed. In one incident a gun and a long knife were found in the Traffic Police garage. Apparently, these weapons were left by some drivers who were being ticketed. Various departments seemed to have been victims of fear as observed by Kauko Aromaa, a Finnish researcher (1990).

An official publication of the Helsinki Police Department (1986) explained why "neighborhood police operations" were necessary. The migration of the population from the countryside to the major urban centers had weakened the "close control of the community." As a result, "the quality of order and safety has deteriorated." According to a "more pessimistic prediction, a Westerner, accustomed to affluence, will become nonchalant, egotistical, shallow and alienated. Violence will grow to such an extent that a police state with strict control will emerge." A publication of the Tampere Police Department (1980) described their "territorial police operations" to the public and stated that "some important structural changes have been taking place in our society," resulting in "a growth in criminal activities." It added that "the rapid growth of crime and inadequate police resources" were responsible for the centralization of police services.

Finns have historically witnessed acts of public violence. Around 1400 a Catholic bishop was killed by "a Finnish chieftain" (Wuorinen, 1965). When the "Russification of Finland for the sake of Russification" was begun by the Czar's representative, Governor General Bobrikov, he was shot to death in 1904 by a young Finn who "became a national hero" (Jutikkala, 1962). After the civil war in 1918 (Silenti,1990), the victorious Whites put "75,000 Red prisoners in concentration camps and 12,000 of them died." "No pity was felt for the prisoners ... because they were considered guilty of having fought against the most precious possession of the nation, its independence" (Jutikkala, 1962). In 1922 the Minister of the Interior of independent Finland was assassinated for political reasons. Violent death through suicide is a national problem (Lonnqvist, 1977). Annually, approximately 50,000 drunks are arrested by the police in Helsinki; some of them indulge in violence. Although Finland has the lowest rate for thefts and narcotic offenses in Scandinavia, "the homicide rate of 3 per 100,000 of population was considered to be high by European standards." Compared to Norway and Denmark, Finland has a rate of assaults "three times higher" but "similar" to that in Sweden (Solsten and Meditz, 1990). Today, "public order is hardly ever threatened, and we have neither serious civil disobedience nor terrorism" (Virta, 1989). In Finnish cities the public transport is efficient and available at all times, and the streets even during the harsh Finnish winters are hardly deserted at any hour. The police perception of hazards in Helsinki and other Finnish cities appeared to be an occupational reaction. As Skolnick (1975) explains, "danger" isolates a police officer mentally from even the conventional citizenry.

Various police officers complained that resources were too meager for them to function efficiently. Resources included personnel, cars, technical equipment like computers, buildings, and recreational facilities. Some patrol officers argued that they did not have enough handcuffs. Shortages of manpower were another major grievance, aggravated by a lack of a rational distribution of human resources. According to the statistics of the Ministry of the Interior (1987),

Helsinki seemed to have an excess of 437 police officers while other important cities like Espoo, Vantaa, and Tampere were short by 137, 118, and 56 officers respectively. A report submitted by a private firm (Mec-Rastor, 1988) stated that police personnel resources were "unevenly distributed." Traditionally, the city police departments had greater share of personnel than the rural districts. The original determination of personnel had been done on the basis of population, but the large migration in the country from the North to the South after World War II had affected allocations. Soisten and Meditz (1990) mention that "the postwar economic transformation that caused even a larger movement of people within Finland, a movement known to Finns as the Great Migration," added 412,000 people to the population of Helsinki and its surroundings. In addition to police manpower allocations not being affected by population growth, Finnish police manpower distribution was not based on "the amount of various tasks to be performed by the police departments." A survey conducted by the same consulting firm (1988) stated that the police were aware that "the manpower and other resources of the police were too restricted."

Finnish officers maintained that in addition to shift work and the job hazards, the police salary was not attractive to officers at junior levels. Rural police chiefs and other senior police officers said that they made good money. "The salary of state employees is regulated by law and degree," and senior officers were entitled to "age increments and high costs of living supplements." Recently work had been "narrowed," and "the salaries of some groups of civil servants, particularly at the highest levels, were raised substantially" (Nousiainen, 1971). Analyzed in terms of Herzberg's (Souryal, 1977) motivation and hygiene factors, the complaints were mainly in regard to the latter. Officers thought working conditions, money, and security were somewhat inadequate, although they seemed motivated by future achievement, recognition, and challenges at work. These motivators were the same factors that motivated these officers when they had joined the police. However, in 1976 the police had gone on a seventeen-day strike over "the level of earning and the conditions on the job" (Makinen and

195

Takala). In 2000, a rare police demonstration was seen in Helsinki, the purpose of which was to catch attention on the salary and limited resources of the police.

Most officers had no objection to working with civilians in the department. Some expressed misgivings about these workers, because they could divulge police secrets. However, some police officers complained that some of their own colleagues talked about the secrets of their trade. A widespread belief existed that police work was secret. It was apparently fostered because much of the reading material given to officers was marked, "police use only." Treating police work as a secret may create problems, as Manning (1978) has noted.

Police would like many of their jobs to be given to civilian employees. They included guarding embassies, cells for drunks or *putka,* jails *or poliisivankila,* and courts. They also disliked driving at the Ministries, serving notices or *haastaminen,* and transporting prisoners and drunks.

Finnish police and their environment

Police officers wanted the public to cooperate with them fully and actively by keeping them informed of all suspicious activities. Some wanted the public to inform the police specifically about their expectations. Only a few wanted directives from the public as to how police priorities should be fixed. A delicate balance must be achieved between police professionalism as conceived by police officers and the extent they should be directed by the public in the formulation and implementation of their tasks. Although the police must be responsive to public needs, their professionalism, they feel, would be jeopardized if their expertise was not given full recognition to allow them to conduct their functions independently. The police must remain accountable to the public, although they may have autonomy in their operation.

Within the centralized, national police bureaucracy of Finland, a responsible spirit of accountability to the public would have to be generated by the police leadership. Unlike England or the U.S., in Finland opportunities exist to bureaucratically shield the police from direct public criticism. However, Finnish police have positive attitudes toward the public who think highly of their police. In surveys conducted by Mec-Rastor, (1988), judges and university professors speak well of the police. As Geller *(1985)* states, the issues of accountability for American police "are not simple matters," and they are not simple in Finland too. Tornudd (1968) claims that "the principle of equality before law is highly valued in our society," and consequently, the police are likely to be discreet and cautious. Rousi (1989) observes that police leaders need to determine "whether or not policing that adheres to the expectations of the general public is competent policing, or whether competence is to be measured by the extent to which the police act strictly in accordance with official regulations." However, in "small countries like Finland, where key decisions may be made within a small group of politicians, administrators and scientific experts interacting with each other" (Tornudd, 1968), public accountability assumes a special importance in democratic decision-making. Moreover, in Finland today "administrative officials have been delegated increasing power in issuing statutes ... the so-called average citizen has begun to divorce himself from government" (Aarnio, 1986). Another observer (Saraviita, 1986) has remarked that the average Finnish citizen "is becoming alienated from the traditional decision making process."

According to the survey of Mec-Rastor (1988) involving 919 respondents of all ages and occupations in Tampere and its neighborhood, the public in Finland have "a positive attitude" toward the police. They were not "afraid" of the police, and contacting them was not difficult. Police officers did not interfere excessively with peoples' lives. On a scale of four to ten, the police received 7.4, or a "satisfactory" rating. The survey reveals that "the higher the age of the respondents, the more positive was the score received by the police." Public dissatisfaction existed over a perceived lack of police resources to control drugs, professional crime, and drunken drivers. In particular, senior citizens suffered from a sense of insecurity in the evenings and weekends. It was felt that the police did not seem very concerned about preventing street violence; foot patrols were few; drunken driving was not treated firmly by the police. Respondents claimed that more attention was paid to the criminal's right than to those of the victim. Investigation was considered time-consuming. The public felt that the police would be lenient toward the criminals occupying established positions in society. Young people complained, "different police officers treated different people differently. However, the police were also considered "efficient" and "willing to serve."

From their responses, Finnish police are healthily sensitive to the media. They consider the media to be fairly positive about the coverage of police activities. Most officers seem to condemn the few sensational newspapers as being too commercial and devoid of ethical standards in their reports of certain police actions. Unethical reports can mislead the public and cause misunderstanding about the role of the police.

Some officers felt that some government agencies responsible for allocation of state resources were unable to appreciate police problems, needs, and demands. They attribute the reasons for the scarcity of police equipment and manpower to a lack of understanding by these agencies. Some officers thought the limited resources of the police reflect the lack of wealth in the nation.

Like American police who claim that courts make it difficult for them to control crime because of their liberal attitudes toward the rights of criminals (Radelet, 1986), the police in Finland felt that the courts and the prison department were somewhat liberal. Police reaction is understandable, because they are exposed to the political heat generated by public criticism, adverse media publicity, and victims' resentment.

Police officers seem to look upon their environment as supportive. There were no we-they attitudes which are mentioned profusely in the discussion of police subculture in America (Westly, 1978; Neiderhoffer, 1974; Drummond 1976; Bedrosian, 1985). The officers seem proud of the excellent qualities of their force which, they think, reflect the Finnish virtues. They feel the police are without deviance, about which a great deal of research has been done in America, England, and Australia (Barker and Carter, 1986; Punch, 1985; Heffernan and

Stoup, 1985; Harrison, 1987).

Political influence

Aware of their vulnerability as frontline workers in the administration of criminal law, the police do not complain of being politically vulnerable in Finland. Politicians do not attempt to influence the police. Many officers believe that personal political influence may exist for police leaders, but most Finnish policemen and women, officers maintain, are above political manipulation that is not a tradition in Finland. If the unequal distribution of police resources among various police units continues and if the police feel that certain government agencies do not appreciate their problems, political lobbying may begin. Many officers including senior leaders thought they could resist political influence.

However, active politics is not forbidden for Finnish police. Police officers get elected as Members of Parliament. Police officers including police chiefs or rural police chiefs occupy important elected positions in city or county councils. Finnish police, however, pride themselves on their political neutrality, and like their countrymen, officers say that their political views are private matters. They have had a phobia of being politically involved. As an undated official publication of Finnish police stated:

> This, however, did not immediately result in any improvement in the handling of police affairs, as witnessed by a declaration of the Ministry of Justice in 1906 to the effect that there were shortcomings in the police and that *even politics had interfered in police operations* (stress added).

Nevertheless, Vartola (1988) noted that party politics "has increased within the administration both of the State and of the municipalities, particularly from the 1960s." Appointments for which the "essential basis of selection has been party affiliation" are frequently made, and one hears "imprecise talk of 'representative bureaucracy' and ... the need for politically guiding the administration under changed circumstances" through "political appointments."

Nousiainen (1971) observes that after World War II, the highest administrative posts have been filled "with an eye to an individual's party affiliation and his merits in party politics." He observes that it is "difficult" to determine "to what degree political factors are influential in appointments made at the base of the administrative pyramid." Nousiainen suggests that politicization does not seem to have led to the selection of people without "the substantive competence required for the appointment." It is held that "political experience can in some posts nicely supplement experience which is purely administrative."

Most police officers agreed that no organized groups oppose the police in Finland. A few officers mentioned individuals, previously maltreated by some officers at one time or the other, who may think all police officers are unfair. Such people may carry negative opinions about the police. Generally, young people, particularly those under fifteen years of age who are not legally liable for violations of the laws, seem opposed to the police. Other groups mentioned include the Gypsies, leftist parties, members of the Green Party, and criminals. Also, during 1990s, the animal activists have been in confrontation with the police, and criminal motorcycle groups have increased their visibility in the society.

Finnish police seem correct in their perception that no organized opposition to the police exists. In the parliamentary proceedings of Finland, no critical references are made about the police. An incomplete project (Gronfors, 1989) finds that young Finns think well of the police. In prisons, inmates expressed only a few minor complaints against the police about their locking handcuffs tightly or using abusive language. Virta (1989) remarks that "consensual politics," a lack of "pluralism in society," the "high degree of legitimacy" enjoyed by the police, the absence of terrorism and civil disobedience, and threats to "public order' have resulted in "low policing" which is basically "routine law enforcement and street-level order maintenance."

National values and legal workers

Police officers state that the most common values respected in their communities are honesty, patriotism, truthfulness, professional skills, calmness, and devotion to family. According to them, most of their police colleagues also exhibit these values, as do good Finns.

The qualities observed by police officers in their organization are reliability, impartiality, and friendliness. Banton (1964) observed that English police were as respectable as the church and the monarchy. Although Finnish police are not probably claiming that kind of respectability, their estimate of the virtues of their colleagues and organization is reminiscent of Banton's comparison. Their pride and self-respect resemble that of the Japanese police (Bayley, 1976). Almost all thought of themselves first as Finnish police and second as members of their unit. The exceptions were mostly the Traffic Police who function as a distinct unit. In addition to controlling traffic on highways, they act as "the reserve police of the state" and help other police units "maintain order and safety as well as prevent crime" (*Liikkuva Poliisi*). No officers were interviewed from the *Keskusrikospoliisi* or NBI which functions as a separate central agency responsible for the investigation of serious offenses. Five provinces govern the police in the country, and "a provincial government is, first of all, the highest police authority in a province" (Nousiainen, 1971). However, the police do not feel that they belong to a particular province; police officers have their own Finnish spirit and sense of homogeneity. Perhaps the centralized training and the existence of the Supreme Police Command and the size of the country contribute to the unique bonds of police brotherhood.

Police officers in Finland seem generally satisfied with the powers given to them by laws. Some felt their powers were reduced as a result of the new Pre-Trial Investigation Law or *Esitutkintalaki* which would erode their effectiveness against crime. Many police officers were concerned that more law reforms (Lahti, 1985) in Finland would occur. Finland's criminal code was established in 1889

(Joutsen, 1987). Most parts of the Criminal Law/Penal Code have been renewed during 1990s. More powers, like the right to intercept telephone conversations and to take legal action against juveniles under fifteen years of age, were sought by police officers from all units. However, they emphasized that the enhanced powers were needed by the detective branch or *Rikospoliisi*. Telephone interception powers, they thought, were required in drug cases. Telephone surveillance and the right to listen to phone calls in serious crime cases, mainly drug crime, white-collar crime and money laundering, has already been gained. In 2001, the police also finally gained the claimed right to under cover actions and feigned purchase in certain serious crime cases.

Almost all officers remarked that criminals and suspects had sufficient rights, but they would not like those rights to be revoked. They recommended that suspects and criminals should have legal rights in the interest of human rights to uphold the rule of law and to maintain the Finnish tradition that their society was based upon law.

Finland has "deep-rooted traditions of ... human rights" (Lehtimaja, 1977). Safeguards provided to the accused include the non-admissibility of statements made to the police as full evidence, the legal obligation of investigators to pay equal attention to the presentation of evidence showing both the guilt and innocence of a suspect, and the right of a suspect to ask the police to instigate further investigation if what has been done is unsatisfactory. Although evidence obtained "illegally" can be used in court, police officers responsible for such illegality are liable for prosecution. Along with the renewal of the jurisdictional districts, these tasks of the police and the prosecutors were divided between two separate office holders. No provision exists for bail in the country. No habeas corpus exists against abusive confinement in Finland, although an aggrieved party may appeal to the Chancellor of Justice or the Parliamentary Ombudsman. As Lehtimaja states, Finland has developed its own unique system of legal safeguards:

202

The chiefs of local police are often graduates in law, well-versed in the rules of criminal procedure and having practical judicial experience as part of their legal training. Indeed many of them identify themselves as jurists rather than police officers. Even lay people call them (as well as all graduates in law) with the title of judge. In fact, some of them make a combined career of the Bench and the Police, shifting from one to the other.

Although individual officers of some units may receive gifts on special occasions, no systematic taking or demanding of gifts by the police exists in Finland. Bribery was almost unknown. Some officers had been offered money by drivers in traffic situations, but such offers cause trouble for the drivers. Physical or verbal abuse is not unknown, but officers do not consider it a problem. Alcohol abuse is not a problem, and police officers say that only about 5 percent of the force could be affected by it. Manipulation of the law in crime fighting and moonlighting were considered very minor problems.

Finnish police officers found it difficult to explain why their colleagues had such high standards of behavior. As Finns, they found that honesty was a way of life with them. Some mentioned their moral upbringing at home, their self-pride, and their character. Curiously, they thought it was almost beneath their dignity to say that they had acquired moral values like the avoidance of force as far as practicable, developing consumer-style relationships with the public, the cultivation of persuasive skills, and a sense of impartiality had been cultivated during their pre-service training. Pride, honesty, and morality seem to have endowed Finnish police with a high sense of moral and psychological well-being. Few officers mentioned the Chancellor of Justice and Parliamentary Ombudsman, "the two organs supervising the legality of the actions of all tribunals and public agencies" (Hiden, 1968; Kastari, 1965) as helping them avoid dishonest methods.

In the annual reports of "the Parliamentary Ombudsman" from 1983 to 1988, some complaints against the police included arrest without sufficient evidence, detention of a prisoner longer than necessary, illumination at night of occupied police cells, denial of rights to prisoners, not providing prisoners with a copy of the Ministry of Interior's instructions on how to treat them, lack of proper training to prevent occasional prisoner deaths, denial to access to public information, failure to record in investigation reports favorable information about an accused, severe treatment of mentally ill or intoxicated people, excessive restriction in handling a protest, denial of proper legal rights to an alien at an international airport, denial of visiting rights to a parent of a child, manhandling a juvenile offender, and an unlawful search of a home. In one annual report (1986) two police officers were "deemed to have acted in an unsuitable manner in accepting positions as guards in a municipal camping ground against the views of their superior." In another annual report (1987) the following appears about a Sheriff or a *Nimismies:*

> A superintendent of the county police was reprimanded because he has acted in violation of his official responsibilities in utilizing his official car of the county police department when participating in training outside of his own county and in attempting to invoice the State for alcohol served at a lunch he hosted for certain spectators at a competition between policemen, even though he had not been allocated such sums in the budget.

According to Laitinen (1986), only ten out of 160,000 civil servants were accused of "receiving bribes" in the 1980s. Based on 400 responses to a questionnaire circulated among civil servants, he remarks that" the majority of the respondents stated that they had either enjoyed or been offered some benefits by outsiders" including meals (84 percent), small gifts or manufacturing samples (21 percent), an evening's entertainment *(50* percent), and "a trip to get acquainted with the matter in hand or for study purposes." Two years later, Laitinen (1988) found a decline in the public's perception of the trustworthiness of public officials. Only 34 percent of adult Finnish citizens trusted "administrative personnel" in 1988 as compared to 53 percent in 1977. However, Laitinen notes emphatically that "most briberies take place between different power institutions" and between top decision-makers in government and businesses and "economic enterprises." He implies that "organizational crime" is increasing.

Views of the future

Officers thought that the government should recognize the demanding as well as hazardous nature of police work. That recognition included increased salaries, sophisticated and reliable equipment, and greater legal powers.

To effect changes, police officers thought they needed to make some changes within their organization. Such changes included the will by the leadership to consider change, greater promotional opportunities, a rational distribution of existing resources, the amalgamation of smaller districts, expansive training and education, and a greater emphasis on physical fitness. Some officers felt that patrol officers, like their counterparts in America as described by Skolnick and Bayley (1986), should have an "input into departmental decisions."

However, the officers generally felt that their profession was improving. No dire need existed to make any changes for the sake of doing something new. They advocated changes that should be deliberate, planned, and supported by the rank-and-file.

Conclusions: Moving away from legalistic policing?

Policing in Finland is a respectable institution, and officers have been traditionally respected. According to a survey made in 1997, 84 percent of the citizens relied on the police. Police honestly is taken for granted; little is heard of police corruption.

Law has historically been important in the affairs of Finland. The police in Finland are accepted with high esteem, because they are regarded as an agency for the administration of the laws of the land. However, Finland's traditional concept of the police as a purely legal institution has some unintended consequences. The notion of the police as an agency for only legal matters has prevented them from socially interacting with people. As Finland becomes increasingly integrated to the European Community, the influx of foreigners, and the growth of a cosmopolitan culture popular among young Finns, the police may have to be socially integrative to reduce the tension produced by the infiltration of new influences.

Because Finns tend to depend on law as an instrument of social agenda, new national legislation may be needed to enlarge the scope of police activity. Although new legislation may help, high morale, lack of corruption, and good public image of Finnish police should help them expand their work to include social activities. The police should try to distance themselves from the legal mode and prepare themselves to become social agents to improve the quality of life. They need to get the public involved in the affairs of the police, and they have a successful example of community police experimentations in the city of Turku. Community policing, or *lahipoliisitoiminta*, has been adopted as the new mode of action for the police and it is nowadays a common practice in several cities.

The police may find encouragement that the Government of Finland wants to withdraw from its traditional bureaucratic ideals. It recognizes that the "administrative machinery has not adjusted well to the needs of the welfare state ... administration has not sufficiently been able to serve its clients" (1987). It realizes that "the purpose of the improvement of public services is to bring the premises, expectations and measures of citizens and offices closer to each other" (Kiviniemi, 1988). Finnish police have a general awareness of the need for crime prevention by involving communities. However, the prevention budget, as it exists at the Supreme Police Command is minimal and is basically for projects aimed at preventing traffic accidents. During 1990s, a massive prevention program against white-collar crime was carried out, and then the emphasis shifted towards drug crime prevention. Also a national program to promote general safety, *Turvallisuustalkoot,* was introduced. The observer author noted that there was an impression in some quarters that the police had remained fundamentally reactive, responding to public requests instead of endeavoring to make people their partners. Their activities remained conceptually, traditionally, and popularly legalistic. A traditional practice has been responsible for retaining the legalistic

206

concept. Every police chief including the rural police chief must be a lawyer with practical training.

But this has changed as one can also see from the account given above. Because the courts have been reorganized to eliminate the distinction between rural and urban centers of justice, the need for law degrees for police chiefs and rural police chiefs is no longer imperative. Now the police officers with commanding officer's degree are able to continue their studies and obtain a university degree, and many of them have already done so.

The police in Finland worried that their legal powers would be eroded with the process of law reforms to make the Finnish criminal law conform to human rights standards in Europe. Police officers felt that their previous power to detain suspects for long interrogations was helpful in obtaining confessions and solving crimes. However, the police in Finland have more powers than their counterparts in many countries; they can keep a suspect in custody for three days. Finnish police should voluntarily surrender some of their powers to provide a democratic and liberal climate. By changing their legalistic culture, the police may seek the cooperation and good will of the public. A voluntary surrender of legal powers and a visible search for partnership with the public would invigorate the police.

Moreover, public and social actions by the police may eliminate some lingering doubts about their just and democratic attributes. The "Finnish state police" (Rautkallio, 1987) have been stigmatized by their past association with the German security police. Another inheritance from the past occurred after Finland became a Grand Duchy of the Czar of Russia and "the municipal Finnish police gradually became a state police when Finland was annexed to Russia in 1809" (Knutsson, Kuhihorn, and Reiss, 1979). Consequently, the police became a state power rather than a democratic institution accountable to people. With an increasing openness to public and social involvement, a willing surrender of those powers that are not in conformity with European standards of human rights, and a decreasing dependence on their legal powers, Finnish police can combine the honesty and integrity of the present with a community and social alliance in the future.

Notes

1. According to a Finnish historian (Alapuro, 1980), "during the Swedish period the most important Finnish center had been Turku." It was where "the university, the throne of the archbishop, and the court of appeal were situated" from the Middle Ages to 1809 when Finland became incorporated into the Russian Empire. Because Turku was "economically and culturally oriented to Sweden," the Czar named Helsinki, a small city, as the capital "to weaken the orientation towards Sweden." It was also situated nearer "St. Petersburg on the southern coast."

2. However, in the first decade of the twenty-first century it is possible for a policeman with a commanding officer's degree granted by the Police College to rise up to all the highest police positions – meaning that police officers who have completed basic police training can become local police chiefs if they have obtained a commanding officer's degree.

3. Quite a few officers mentioned to the observer author that they joined the police, because the preparatory education was mostly free.

References

Aarnio, Aulis. 1986. The Legitimization of Law. In the Institute of Nordic Law, ed. *Juhlakirja*. Rovaniemi, Finland: University of Lapland.

Alapuro, Risto. 1980. *Finland. An Interface Periphery*. Helsinki: Yliopistopaino.

Alestalo, Matti, Rudolf Andorka, and Istvan Harcsa. 1987. *Agricultural Population and Structural Change: A Comparison of Finland and Hungary*. Helsinki: Yliopistopaino.

Alestalo, Matti, Peter Flora, and Hannu Uusitalo. 1985. Structure and Politics in the Making of the Welfare State: Finland in Comparative Perspective. In Risto Alapuro, Matti Alestalo, Elina Haavio-Mannila, and Raimo Vayrynen, eds. *Small States in ComparativePerspective:Essays for Erik Allardt*. Oslo: Norwegian University Press.

Alkio, Olavi, Kari Pitkanen, Heikki Ravantti, and Tapio Vaherva. 1988. *Adult Education in Finland. Helsinki:* Kansanvalistusseura.

Allardt, Erik. *1985. Finnish Society: Relationships between the Geopolitical Situation and the Development of Society*. Helsinki: Yliopistopaino.

Aromaa, Kauko. 1990. Personal Interview. Helsinki.

Baley, David H. 1976. *Forces of Order: Police Behavior in Japan and the United States*. Berkeley: University of California Press.

Balvig, Flemming. 1985. Crime in Scandinavia: Trends, Explanations and Consequences. In Bishop Norman, ed. *Scandinavian Research Council for Criminology* 1980-85.

Banton, Michael. 1964. *The Policeman in the Community*. New York: Basic Books.

Barker, Thomas and David L. Carter. 1986. *Police Deviance*. Cincinnati, OH: Pilgrimage.

Bedrosian, A. 1985. An Occupational Hazard. The Subculture of Police. In Hany W. More, Jr., ed. *Critical Issues in Law Enforcement*. Cincinati, OH: Anderson Publishing Co.

Boydstun, John E. and Michael E. Sherry. 1975. San Diego Community Profile, *Final Report*. Washington D.C.: Police Foundation.

Central Criminal Police. 1987. *Annual Report.* Keskusrikospoliisi Vuosikertomus. Helsinki.

Committee for Improvement of Tactics and Methods. 1987. *A Project to Improve Crime Investigation and the Methods Used in Crime Prevention.* Helsinki.

Drummond, D.S. 1976. *Police Culture.* Beverly Hills, CA: Sage Publications.

Ellonen, Erkki, 1990. Personal Interview. Tampere.

The Finnish Chapter of the International Police Association and the Department for Police Affairs of the Ministry of the Interior. *Police in Finland.* Helsinki: Auranen.

Geller, William A. 1985. *Police Leadership in America: Crisis and Opportunity.* Westport,CT: Frederick A. Praeger.

Goldstein, Herman. 1977. *Policing a Free Society.* Cambridge, MA: Ballinger Publishing Company.

Gronfors, Martti. 1990. Personal Interview. Helsinki.

Finnish Gypsies and the Police, *Scandinavian Studies in Criminology* 7. Olso: Scandinavia University Books.

Harrison, John. 1987. *Police Misconduct: Legal Remedies.* London: Legal Action Group.

Heffernan, William C. and Timoothy Stroop. 1985. *Police Ethics: Hard Choices in Law Enforcement.* New York: The John Jay Press.

Heinanen, Aira; Hannele Kaiponen, and Helena Palojarvi. *1985. Poliisin ja Sosiaalityontekijan Yhteistoimintakokeilu Perhevakivaltatilanteissa I (The First Cooperational Experiment between the Police and Social Workers in Cases of Domestic Violence).* Helsinki: Ensi Kotien Liitto.

Helminen, Klaus. 1989. Personal Correspondence. Otaniemi.

Helsinki Police Department. 1989. Training Design and Layout for 1989. (Koulutussuunnitelma Yuodelle 1989).

1986. *Aluepoliisitoiminnasta Helsingissa* (Territorial Police Operations in Helsinki). Helsinki.

Hiden, Mikael J. V. 1968. Finland's Defenders of Law, *The Annals,* 377, 3 1-40.

Joutsen, Matti. 1989. *The Criminal Justice System of Finland.* Helsinki: Ministry of Justice.

Joutsen, Matti and Raimo Lahti 1997. *Finland.* Monsey, NY: Criminal Justice Press

1987. *The Penal Code of Finland and Related Laws.* Littleton, CO: Fred B. Rothman & Co.

Joutsen, Matti and Jorma Kalske. 1984. *Prosecutorial Decision-Making in Finland.* Helsinki: National Research Institute of Legal Policy.

Jutikkala, Eino. 1962. *A History of Finland.* New York: Frederick A. Praeger, Inc.

Kastari, Paavo. 1965. Finland's Guardians of Law. In Donald C. Rowat, ed. *The Ombudsman.* London: Unwin Brothers Ltd.

Keskusrikospoliisi. 1988. *Vuosikertomus* 1987 (Annual Report 1987). Helsinki: VAPK.

Kirby, David. 1990. Finland. In Stephen Salter and John Stevenson, eds. *The Working Class and Politics in Europe and America,* 1929-1945. New York: Longman Inc.

Kiviniemi, Markku. 1988. *The Improvement of the Public Services.* Helsinki: The Administrative Development Agency.

Knutsson, Johannes, Eckart Kuhihorn, and Albert Reiss, Jr. 1979. The History of The Police Organization in Scandinavia. In Knutsson Johannes, Eckart Kuhlhom, and Albert Reiss, Jr., eds. *Police and Social Order.* Stockholm: Research and Development Division.

Kuisma, Markku. 1989. Civil Service of Finnish Central Administration in 1809-1984: Problems of Socio-Historical Research. In Seppo Tiihonen, ed. *Institutions and Bureaucrats.* Helsinki: Government Printing Centre.

Lahti, Raimo. 1985. Current Trends in Criminal Policy in Scandinavian Countries. In Norman Bishop, ed. *Scandinavian Criminal Policy and Criminology* 1980-1985. Copenhagen: Scandinavian Research Council for Criminology.

Laitinen, Ahti. 1988. *Organizational Crime and Power Institutions.* A paper presented at the Tenth International Congress on Criminology. Hamburg, Germany.

Laitinen, Ahiti. 1994. "Police in Finland" in Dilip Das (Ed.) *Police Practices: An International Review.* Munchen, N.J.: The Scarecrow Press.

1986. Structural Crime in Finland: An Agenda and Model for Research. A paper presented at the World Congress of Sociology. New Delhi.

Lehtimaja, Lauri. 1977. *The Protection of Human Rights in Finnish Criminal Proceedings.* Turku: University of Turku.

Liikkuva, Poliisi. *Liikkuvan Poliisin Tehtävät* (The Tasks of the Mobile Police). Helsinki.

Lonnqvist, Jouko. 1977. *Suicide in Helsinki.* Helsinki: Psychiatric Clinic.

Makinen, Tuija and Takala, Hannu. The 1976 Police Strike in Finland, *Scandinavian Studies in Criminology,* 7, Oslo: Scandinavian University Books.

Manning, Peter K. 1978. Lying, Secrecy, and Social Control. In Peter K. Manning and John Van Maanen, eds. *Policing: A View from the Street.* Santa Monica, CA: Goodyear Publishing Company.

Mantila, Anu. 1988. Community Policing: The Opinions of Neighborhood and District Policemen of Their Work. In Patrick Tormudd, ed. *Research Report Summaries* 1987. Helsinki: VAPK Kampin Valtimo.

Maude, George. 1990. Personal Interview. Turku.

1976 The Finnish Dilemma. London: Oxford University Press.

Mec-Rastor. 1988. Poliisivakanssien Suuntaus: Raportti (Managing Vacancy Distribution within the Police Force. Espoo: Finland.

1988. Tampereen Ja Sen Lahikuntien Asukkaiden Kasitykset Poliisin Toiminnasta (Opinions of the Residents of Tampere and its Suburbs about Police Operations). Espoo:Finland.

Ministry of Finance. 1987. *A Survey of Measures to Develop Administration.* Helsinki, Government Printing Centre, 1987.

Ministry of Interior. 1983. *Ministry of the Interior. 1983.* Helsinki, Government Printing Centre, 1983.

Ministry of Justice. 1983. *Making and Applying Law in Finland.* Hesinki: Government Printing Centre.

National Research Institute of Legal Policy. 1988. *Research Report Summaries.* Helsinki: VAPK.

Niederhoffer, A. 1974. *Behind the Shield.* New York: Doubleday Publishing Company. Nousiainen, Jaakko. 1971. *The Finnish Political System.* Cambridge, MA: Harvard University Press.

The Parliamentary Ombudsman. 1983-1988. *Report of the Parliamentary Ombudsman, Summary,* 1983-1988. Helsinki.

Parker, L. Craig Jr. 1993. *Finnish Criminal Justice: An American Perspective.* Landam, NY: University Press of America.

Pentikainen Juha and Veikko Anttonen. 1985. Finland as a Cultural Area. In Juha Pentikainen and Veikko Anttonen, eds. *Cultural Minorities in Finland: An Overview towards Cultural Policy.* Helsinki: Tilastokirjasto.

Pesonen, Pertti and Onni Rantala. 1985. Outlines of the Finnish Party System. In Risto Alapuro, Matti Alestalo, Elina Haavio-Mannila, and Raimo Vayrynen, eds. *Small States In Comparative Perspectives.* Oslo: Norwegian University Press.

Police Academy. 1987. *Annual Report* (Poliisiopiston Toimintakertomus). Otaniemi.

Police Department, Ministry of Interior. 1987. *A Project to Improve Pretrial Investigation.* Esitutkinnan Kehittamisprojekti. Helsinki.

Poliisikoulu. 1988. *Police School* 1988. Tampere, Finland: Police School.

Poliisin Toiminnan Tunnuslukuja 1987. *(Parameters of Law Enforcement.)* Espoo, Finland.

Project to Improve Pre-trial Investigation. (Esitutkinnan Kehittamisprojekti). 1987. *The Report.* Helsinki: Ministry of Interior.

Punch, Maurice. 1985. *Conduct Unbecoming: The Social Construction of Police Deviance and Control.* London: Tavistock Publications.

1983. *Control in the Police Organization.* Cambridge, MA: The MIT Press.

Radelet, Louis A. 1986. *The Police and the Community.* New York: Macmillan Publishing Company.

Randell, Seppo. 1990. Personal Interview. Tampere.

Rautkallio, Hannu. 1988. *Finland and the Holocaust.* New York: Holocaust Library.

Rousi, Hannele. 1989. The Basis for Research on the Police Profession and Policing in Finland. Unpublished paper. Helsinki.

Ruuska, Kirsti. 1990. Personal Interview, Tampere.

Saraviita, Ilkka. 1986. Special Features of the Planned System of the Referendum in Finland. In the Institute for Nordic Law, ed. *Juhlakirja.* Rovaniemi, Finland: University of Lapland.

Shane, Paul G. 1980. *Police and People: A Comparison of Five Countries.* St. Louis: The C.V. Mosby Company.

Silenti, Tuomo. 1990. A View Point to Finnish Historical Background. Unpublished paper. Helsinki.

Singleton, Fred. 1989. *A Short History of Finland.* New York: Cambridge University Press.

Sinisalo, Kari. 1971. Die Gesetzliche Restlegung der Zuständigkeit der Polizei (The Limits of Police Powers as Based on Law). A thesis. Turku, Finland: University of Turku.

Sisäasiainministerion Poliisiosaston Julkaisusarja. 1987. Esitutkinnan Kehittamisprojekti A *Project to Improve Pretrial Investigation.* Helsinki.

Skolnick, Jerome H. 1975. *Justice without Trial.* New York: John Wiley & Sons.

Skolnick, Jerome H. and David H. Bayley. 1986. *The New Blue Line.* New York: The Free Press, 1986.

Solsten, Eric and Sandra W. Meditz. 1990. *Finland: A Country Study.* Washington D.C.: Government Printing Office.

Souryal, Sam 5. 1977. *Police Administration and Management.* St. Paul: West Publishing Company.

Tampereen Poliisilaitos. 1980. Tampereen Poliisilaitoksen Aluepoliisitominta (TheTerritorial Police Operations within Tampere Police District). Tampere, Finland: Tampere Police Department.

Tapala, I. 1989. *Helsinki Police Department Alarm Center*. Helsinki: Helsinki Police Department.

Tampere Police Department. 1987. *Annual Report.*

Tiihonen, Seppo. 1989. Introduction. In Seppo Tiihonen, ed. *Institutions and Bureaucrats*. Helsinki: Government Printing Centre.

Torke, Hans-Hoachim. 1989. Administration and Bureaucracy in Nineteenth Century Russia: The Empire and the Finnish Case. In Seppo Tiihonen, ed. *Institutions and Bureaucrats*. Helsinki: Government Printing Centre.

Tornudd, Patrick. 1986. *Finland and the International Norms of Human Rights*. Boston: Martinus Nijhoff Publishers.

1968. The Preventive Effect of Fines for Drunkness. *Scandinavian Studies in Criminology*. 2, Oslo: Scandinavia University Books.

1968. A Sombre Mood: The Preventive Effect of Fines for Drunkenness. *Scandinavian Studies in Criminology*, 2, 67-80. Oslo: Scandinavia University Books.

Turku Police Department. 1988. *Handbook of Justice Education. Laillisuuskasvatuksen Kasikirja*. Part 1 and 2. Turku: Police Department.

Turku Summer University (Turun Kesayliopisto). 1988. *The Course Description*. Uusitalo, Paavo. 1990 Personal Interview. Helsinki.

1983. Policing Environmental Conflicts in Finland and Norway: The Structural Basis to the State Reactions to Civil Disobedience. *Disputing Deviance: Experience of Youth in the 80s*. Helsinki: European Group for the Study of Deviance and Social Control.

Valkonen, Tapani. 1990. Personal Interview. Helsinki.

Välitalo, Unto. 1990. Personal Interview. Tampere.

Valtionhallinnon Kehittamiskeskus. 1988. *Julkisen palvelun kuva (The Image of Public Service)*. Helsinki: Kunnallissaatio.

Van Maanen, John. 1978. Kinsmen in Repose: Occupational Perspectives of Policemen. In Peter K. Manning and John Van Maanen, eds. *Policing: A View from the Street*. Santa Monica, CA: Goodyear Publishing Company.

Vartola, Juha. 1988. Finland. In Donald C. Rowat, ed. *Public Administration in Developed Democracies*. New York: Marcel Dekker.

Venna, Yrjo. 1989. Implications of the Public Sector Reform for Management Development in the Finnish Civil Service. Unpublished paper. Helsinki: Administrative Development Agency.

Virta, Sirpa, 1989. Dualism in Policing Policy (Preventive/Repressive Role of the Police). Unpublished paper. Tampere, Finland.

Westley, W.A. 1978. *Violence and the Police*. Cambridge, MA: Harvard University Press.

Wilson, James Q. 1978. *Varieties of Police Behavior*. Cambridge, Massachusetts: Harvard University Press.

Wuorinen, John H. *1965. A History of Finland*. New York: Columbia University Press.

Index